ARCHITECTURE: Bodies of Space

By
Stephen Alton

Introduction by
Livio Dimitriu

USA BOOKS | UNIVERSALIA PUBLISHERS
New York / Verona / Bucharest

STEPHEN ALTON / ARCHITECTURE: BODIES OF SPACE

New York / Verona / Bucharest

Urban Studies & Architecture Books
Universalia Publishers USA

270 Park Avenue South, Suite 4D
NYC, NY, 10010, USA

Tel/Fax: 212-979-5057
E-mail: Ldusainst@aol.com
www.usainstitute.org

Editor
Dr. Livio Dimitriu

Consultants
Vincenzo Pavan

Graphic Design
USA Books, NYC/USA
Studio Mirandola/Cerea, (VR), Italy

Digital Processing
SAA PC, NYC/USA

Drawings / Photo Credits
Drawings courtesy of Stephen Alton Architect, P.C.
All photos by Eduard Hueber, except Enzo and Raffaello Bassotto/pp 8, Paul Warchol/pp 31-32, Barbel Miebach/pp 47-49

Cover Design
Evan Gaffney Design/NYC, USA

Copyright © 2005 by USA BOOKS/Urban Studies & Architecture Books, NYC/USA

International distribution rights belong exclusively to USA Books/Urban Studies & Architecture Books

All right reserved. No part of this book may be reproduced or transmitted in any form or by any means of electronic or mechanical reproduction, including photocopying, recording, and any information storage and retrieval system without written permission from the publisher.

First Edition, 2005, printed and bound in Italy
ISBN 973-86038-9-7

STEPHEN ALTON / ARCHITECTURE: BODIES OF SPACE

CONTENTS

5	**Livio Dimitriu**	Architecture:
	Introduction	Bodies of Space and Tattooed Skins
	PROJECTS	
9	**Residential Buildings**	Atlas New York
		New Gotham
21	**Boutiques**	Mare Shoes
		Donna Karan
		Royale Cards and Gifts
		Sacco Shoes
		Ligne Roset
33	**Private Residences**	Apartment 22
		Apartment 11
		Dual Space: Loft
		Art Port: House Addition
		Other Interiors
53	**Housing and Other Studies**	Concept Restaurant
		Astor
		The Hudson Tea Building "A"
		Hotel Villa La Angostura
68	**Firm Profile**	Stephen Alton Architect, P.C.
		Awards/TV/Publications
		Credits

STEPHEN ALTON / ARCHITECTURE: BODIES OF SPACE

This volume is dedicated to:

All those who had chanced to offer their resources and talent to the likes of me: patrons, educators, and contributors. You are my friends.

Louis Miano and Warren Pearl, without your blind faith and help, reality for me would be very different today.

Allen Prusis, your wisdom and criticism in both good and bad times will never be forgotten.

Michael, Masako, Natalia, Aline, Ade, Kenneth, and Jason, you have all contributed greatly to my work.

Rodolpho Machado, you are a truly an architect and educator that has forever changed the way I see the world.

INTRODUCTION

Livio Dimitriu

On Stephen Alton
Architecture: Bodies of Space and Tattooed Skins

In the work of the New York architect Stephen Alton, space does not mimic the body that inhabits it. Space is the body itself, an independent and all-accepting one. Alton's architecture is a succession of propositions involving the ineffable presence of bodies of space, tattooed and perforated skins, uprooted viewers and inhabitants, that blur the difference between objects and beings, and allows one to become another. These themes are harmonious with the architecture architecture that involve retail stores, residential building, and private residences. Beyond functional concerns, the problem consists in identifying the new, the unexpected, and occasionally the strange as well.

Alton is not concerned with style. The "signature" of his architecture resides with the approach to problem solving. His interest in the recent tradition and architecture history acts as only a source of forms of order that deserve attention. The functional programs that he works with often involve fashion. Alton understands that the Baudelairean "mode," French for "fashion," has been incorporated from early on and in an act of superficial cultural consumerism within the very name of the *Modern Movement*, drifting rapidly away from its earlier connotations of craft and manner of execution. The nineteenth century is valued by the architect for its rigorous system of research. As with the *Beaux Arts* tradition of systematically studying the human body, Alton examines the bodies of space in his architecture by actively taking it through various filters of decomposition. The space describes itself as an image at first, then proceeds to peel off the skin to arrive at an *écorché*, after which it further unfolds to reveal its skeleton, its structure and structuring.

Each and every project is an essay in the study of space: its skin, its muscle, and its bones. This is very much in the spirit of a sculptor's education. Constantin Brancusi, one of the fathers of modern sculpture, patiently examined the human body in his early career, as evidenced by the very well known *écorché* study of a young man's body of 1901, executed while a student at the *Craiova School of Arts and Crafts*. This "object" has never been critically incorporated in any analysis of Brancusi's work to date, even though it is essential for an understanding of how Brancusi dealt with space stripped bare, form, and meaning for the rest of his life. Whatever happened to the skin once removed from the body of space?

For Brancusi, as well as for architects such as Mies van der Rohe, the "skin" returns as an obsession. For Brancusi, the return involved primarily reflective surfaces. For Mies, the glass of the curtain wall is equally a reflective skin. But the architect, like others of his contemporaries, became prey to a formal *dictum* of the *Modern Movement* and attempted to express the structure, thus the skeleton, of the architectonic body in its very skin. This exoskeletal approach to the making of architecture is inconsistent with nature's own rejection of this solution, deemed to be an evolutionary dead end.

Stephen Alton's bodies of space offer an intriguing variation of what might have happened to the skin. The skin becomes the messenger that speaks to the senses beyond the eye and the mind's eye. The skin is tactile and even auditory, as in the sensorial environment of the *Atlas* project. A thin membrane forms the most direct and immediate contact between the architecture and man, whether it is a plane of water, a plane of lacy natural stone corroded by light to the point of appearing immaterial, or the memory of a fabric transformed by photographic media. Alton's concern resides systematically and in all of his projects with tattooing the skins of his architecture with tectonic texts of surface, light, color, sound, and materials. There is no pastiche involved in this is. It is a love learned from and shared with the great masters of the *Modern Movement*, particularly Alvar Aalto and Carlo Scarpa.

Alton's interest in body and skin avoids the rampant consumerism and gratuitous hedonism of much of today's architecture. He is not interested in the derangement of the senses proposed by Rimbaud, but in a rearrangement of the senses more in line with the by-now-traditional stance of Italian *Rationalism* as opposed to the dogma of the fundamentally French *Modern Movement.*

The tattooing of the skins in Alton's architecture involves the writing of an invisible text containing each project's manifesto. There is a certain degree of rhetoric involved in such gestures, as the reference seems in line with Kafka's torture machine in the short story "The Penal Colony." For Kafka, the writing of the text on the human body speaks of the author's obsession and pain brought on by the act of making. For Alton, the intentions "written" on the bodies of space and on the removed "skins" form the surfaces of choice that carry the architectonic text. The floated, levitated ceiling in the *Mare Boutique* acquires autonomy not only on account of its independence in three dimensions but also because of the articulations it exhibits, the way it reveals what is beyond itself, such as the existing capital of a column, how it does not touch the walls, or how it constantly modulates and remeasures the section of the space as one moves into and through the project. Despite the rich readings possible in a project such as *Mare*, in the end it is the understanding and control of one of the most effective tools of design in interior architecture, the ceiling, that impresses most in Alton's sensibility.

The free-floating tattooed ceiling of *Mare* returns as a theme in other projects, such as the free wall of the *Royale Cards and Gifts* store. It is the autonomy of vertically articulated space that interests Alton. Where in *Mare* it was the architect's will that gave shape to the articulation that characterizes the free plane, in *Royale* the material itself, perforated metal, stands on its own for its ready-made quality while participating in the dematerializing of the skin. The architect's intervention consists in selecting the tectonics of the place. This takes courage and integrity in a day and age dominated by ever-increasing architects' egos imposing architectonics disconnected from the substance of space, its materials, and how these serve the function of the project in its broadest and most comprehensive definition. There is a quiet appropriateness of architectonic and tectonic gestures in Alton's architecture that is sufficient to reveal intention and address function without either intellectual or budgetary waste.

Atlas is perhaps the most complex statement produced by Alton to date. It gathers the architect's position and intentions and it adds surprising twists to space making. The various boutiques by Alton have a relationship with the street and the passerby that rely largely on the luminosity of the interior space as perceived at night. Alton speculates here on another position of inter-bellum architecture as proposed by the influential editor *Hoepli* in Milan, when he comissioned a volume entitled *Architetture luminose*. The publication involved exclusively night photos of most of the icon buildings of the *Modern Movement*. Alton's facades rely often on the power of architecture transfigured by artificial light at night, and drawn with light. The skin of the street facade in *Atlas* is tattooed with light at night, so that it reveals the inside as seen from the street and, alternatively, it offers city postcards to the occupants of the lobby. The elliptical floor pattern in the lobby was carefully calibrated so that it would be perceived as a circle in perspective. The *Modern Movement* often professed a naive interest in pure shapes that is a far cry from the sophisticated concern with in the perception of pure space characteristic of all great architecture. The idea of "perfection" in the built ellipse of the *Roman Theater* in Verona proposes that a space ought to be perceived as cylindrical when entered significantly from *The Imperial Gate*. One wonders why the precepts of modernism betrayed the primacy of perception. To build pure shapes, necessarily distorted by perspective, became preferred to the building of compound shapes that are perceived as pure in actual experience. The relationship to theater does not stop here. The perforated facade at *Atlas* performs in the best tradition of the avant-garde experimentation of storefront theater in New York, where the occupants of the street and those of the architecture find themselves blurring the definitions of audience vs. actors, of private vs. public, of urban space vs. interior space. The *Atlas* project hovers in the shadow of Antonin Artaud's theater of cruelty. The facades as well as the interior events in Alton's architecture often confess their voyeuristic nature.

For Alton, to dematerialize also means to levitate, as in the case of the reception desk for the *New Gotham*, or in the light box of the *Mare Shoes Boutique*. The disengagement of the object from its surrounding becomes the very motif of the *Sacco Shoes Boutique*, and runs as a theme through the *Seidmon Residence* and the *Apartment 22/Dlutowski and Occolovitz Residence*. In these projects, migratory objects and nomadic installations provide a subtext founded on the extraordinarily rich Latin etymology for the word "furniture." The "mobile" furniture involves uprooted and noncontextual objects juxtaposed to the "stabile," connotative of the permanence of built architecture. In the *Krug and Haubrich Residence*, the automobile as the epitome of mobility is recognized as "furniture," and art itself is considered in contemporary terms as a transient occupier and definer of space. The bodies of space become the *locus* for the occasional visitors, objects and beings alike. The *Ligne Roset Furniture Showroom* proposes a variation on the theme of freeing the occupants of their space. Here, the color of the objects is ever-changing when perceived from the theater of the street. Subtle gestures reverse normality, such as when a source of light built into the floor has the power to disengage the spatially heavy element of a cast translucent sink from its surroundings in the *Apartment 22*.

The condition of working in the metropolis ultimately means to confront the condition of impermanence characteristic of today's architecture. To uproot, to decontextualize and defamiliarize, to become involved with the transitory, the migratory and the nomadic, are now given conditions of life and architecture. Stephen Alton's work is based on the insistence to build and be concerned with the timeless themes of the bodies of space and the well-tempered craft of their floating skins. This architecture aspires to provide the reassuring missing link to a world of certainties that seems to be long gone. Architecture thus can claim to civilize still the world we live in.

About Livio Dimitriu:
Dr. Livio Dimitriu is an architect practicing in New York, Europe, and Asia, with the award-winning firm *Livio Dimitriu, Inc*. He is the President of *USA Institute* since 1978, an international noprofit research, education, and public-service organization based at the Palazzo Giusti del Giardino in Verona/Italy, and in New York City. Dimitriu is the President of *USA Books*, the senio international editor of *Architext Design Magazine*, and is on the permanent board of editors for *Controspazio Magazine* in Rome/Italy. Prof. Dimitriu is a widely published architect and architecture critic. He taught at over two dozens universities in the Americas, Europe, and Asia, and is a Professor of Architecture at Pratt Institute.

PROJECTS

10 STEPHEN ALTON / ARCHITECTURE: BODIES OF SPACE

STEPHEN ALTON / ARCHITECTURE: BODIES OF SPACE

PROJECT **Atlas New York**
66 West 38th Street, New York City

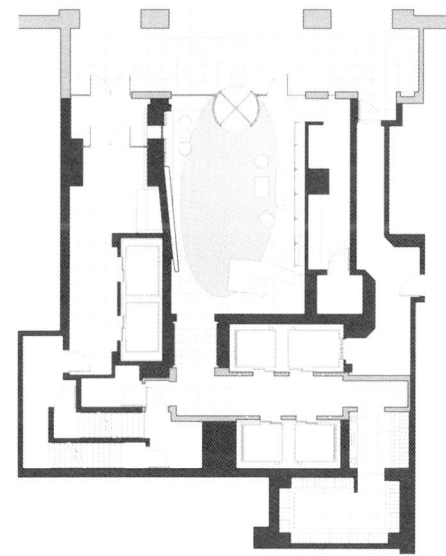

1. Atlas New York. Wall lighting at elevator lobby, pp 9
2. Atlas New York. Street facade, previous page
3. Atlas New York. Plan

Atlas New York is located one block from New York City's fashion epicenter, Bryant Park. The new construction is a mixed-use apartment and office building designed for young fashion-conscious New Yorkers. The project involved interventions on the exterior facade at street level, the lobbies, elevators, internal circulation experiences, the lounge and the gym.

The project explores dialogues among art, artifact, and architecture. The methodology is intended to accentuate the transparent and translucent material "skins" employed, both literally and conceptually, and it underlines the theaterlike voyeurism characteristic of the relationship between street life and life inside New York's buildings. Photography, paintings, and paint are regarded as "construction materials" for the spaces of both the main and the secondary lobbies. "Frames" and framed views alternatively come to the fore and recede relative to the physical walls, their color, and architect-generated paintings. All the elements are juxtaposed with projected and backlighted, fabriclike photographic images. The nature of each spatial layer, both of construction and perception, is intended as a systematic allusion to the fabric and cloth of the *Fashion District*.

The promenade from the street to the building's core involves a sequence of spaces gradually extricated from the noise of the city, colors and textures. The palette of the outer lobby is conceived as an "urban theater" followed by a gray stone threshold chamber where the murmur of running water drowns the city noise. The hazy glow of blue light adds to the otherworldliness of the inner lobby. The walls shift from strong colors to gray and white. The large photo projection of a lace-covered woman's body generates the choice of the lacelike veining for the Italian marble that covers the walls. The sensuality of the human body becomes linked to bodies of space, commenting on the ambiguity between skin and fabric, and between that which is "to cover" and that which is "to reveal." The glossy white interior of the elevators strips the space bare.

12   STEPHEN ALTON / ARCHITECTURE: BODIES OF SPACE

4.

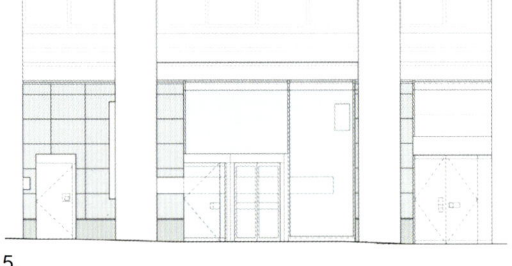

5.

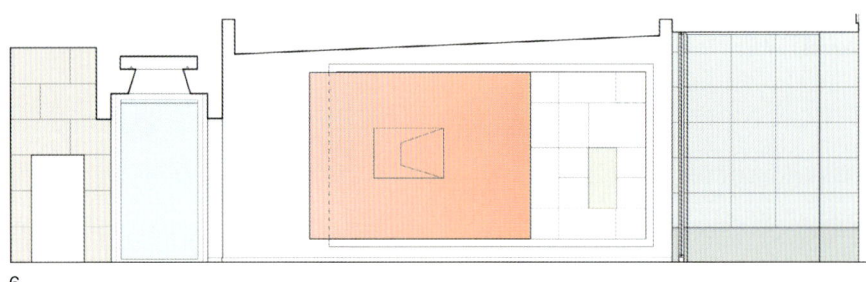

6.

STEPHEN ALTON / ARCHITECTURE: BODIES OF SPACE

7.

4. Atlas New York. View from entry with projected light on red wall and opposite light box wall
5. Atlas New York. Exterior street elevation at entry
6. Atlas New York. Interior section/ elevation through lobbies
7. Atlas New York. View of main lobby towards street
8. Atlas New York. Interior section/ elevation through lobbies
9. Atlas New York. Interior elevation at elevator lobby

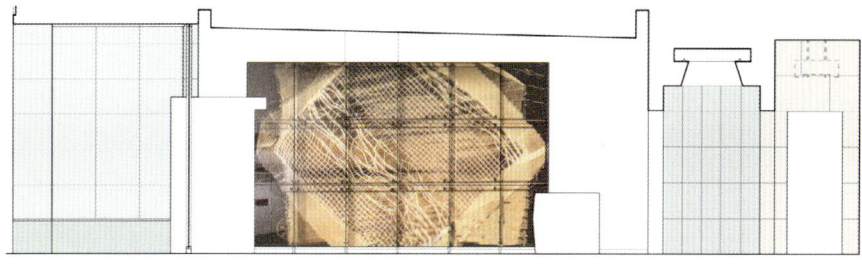

8.

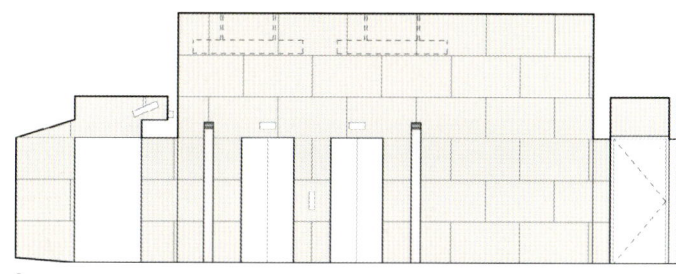

9.

STEPHEN ALTON / ARCHITECTURE: BODIES OF SPACE

10.

11.

10. Atlas New York. Main lobby articulated mirror wall with window
11. Atlas New York. Main floor elevator lobby, Carrara marble skin, back-lit marble, and projection of Yves Saint Laurent dress
12. Atlas New York. Water fall room: Transition space between main lobby and elevator lobby
13. Atlas New York. Office lobby
16. Atlas New York. Second floor lounge with custom table

STEPHEN ALTON / ARCHITECTURE: BODIES OF SPACE

12. 13.

14.

STEPHEN ALTON / ARCHITECTURE: BODIES OF SPACE

PROJECT **New Gotham**
520 West 43rd Street, New York City

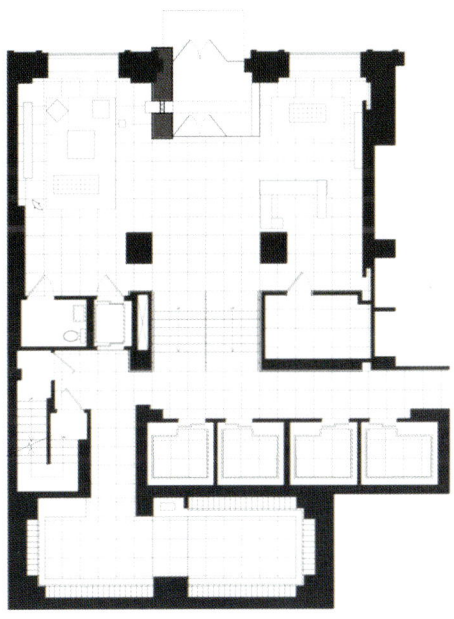

This midtown residential building caters to the younger generation's views on design. The new facade and canopy at street level signal an extension of the urban event into the volume of the building and its lobby space. The traditional motif of the exterior monumental stair was shifted exclusively to the semipublic domain of the main lobby. The gesture declares the modern urban character of the interior, in the spirit of Marcel Breuer's position with regard to the public character of the Whitney Museum lobby. The project established a high design standard for this New York neighborhood at the time of its completion. The lobby stair formally "peels off" the artificial skin of the city, allows the lobby to become a new levitated urban ground at the raised elevator bank, and extends the idea of the city plane all the way into the health club and other related functions.

This award-winning project uses light, materials, and various architectonic elements to activate space through a compositional strategy of constantly and systematically disconnecting volume and planes from one another.

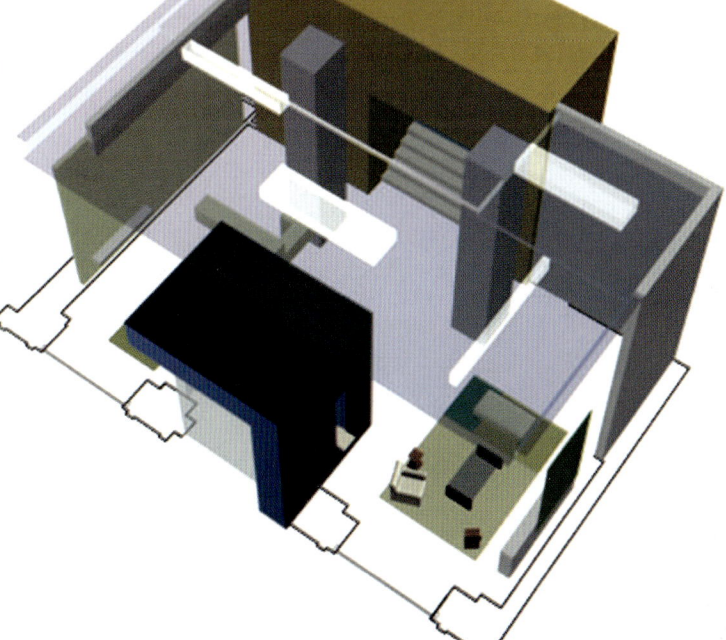

15. New Gotham. Street facade in steel and glass, pp 16
16. New Gotham. Plan of the main lobby
17. New Gotham. Main lobby axonometric

STEPHEN ALTON / ARCHITECTURE: BODIES OF SPACE

18.

19.

18. New Gotham. Main lobby, concierge desk, metal frame and linen-covered box
19. New Gotham. Main lobby concierge desk
20. New Gotham. Main lobby, composite stone floor and metal vestibule
21. New Gotham. Main lobby, view towards elevator bank
22. New Gotham. Basketball/Gym with scrim protector
23. New Gotham. Gym with children's play area
24. New Gotham. Main lobby, pearwood panels, stone floors, concrete panels, and decorative paint

STEPHEN ALTON / ARCHITECTURE: BODIES OF SPACE 19

20.

21.

22.

23.

20 STEPHEN ALTON / ARCHITECTURE: BODIES OF SPACE

25. New Gotham. Seating area with custom sofa and rugs, Fortuny factory lamp and Noguchi hanging lamp

STEPHEN ALTON / ARCHITECTURE: BODIES OF SPACE

PROJECTS **Boutiques**

Mare Shoes
Donna Karan
Royale Cards and Gifts
Sacco Shoes
Ligne Roset

STEPHEN ALTON / ARCHITECTURE: BODIES OF SPACE

27.

28.

26. Mare Shoes. View with floating ceiling, previous pp 21
27. Mare Shoes. Sales Counter with back-lit wall, glass, steel and painted wood
28. Mare Shoes. Display shelves
29. Mare Shoes. Section/elevation
30. Mare Shoes. Section/elevation
31. Mare Shoes. Ceiling detail with skin pierced by existing column
32. Mare Shoes. Plan
33. Mare Shoes. Section/elevation

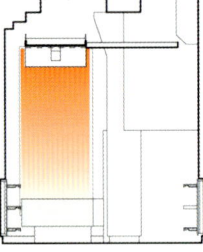

29.

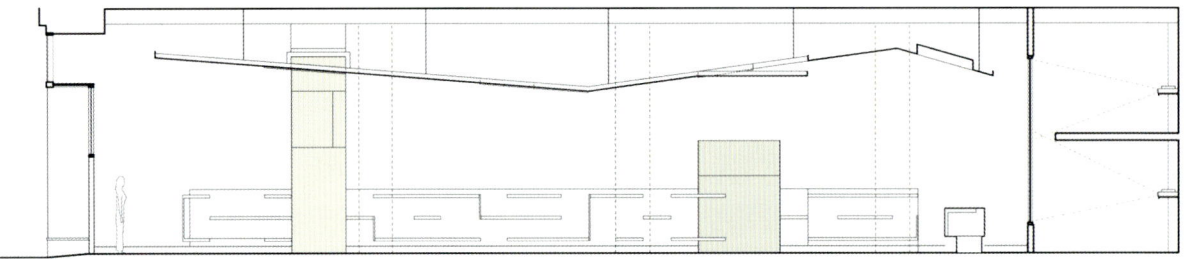

30.

STEPHEN ALTON / ARCHITECTURE: BODIES OF SPACE

31.

PROJECT **Mare Shoes**
100 Fifth Avenue, New York City

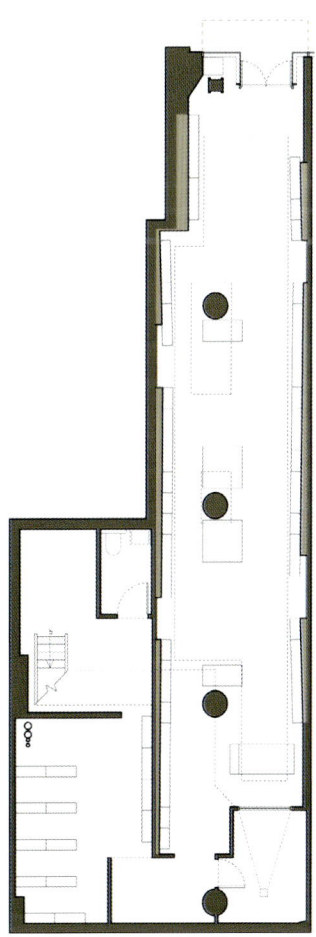

Mare Shoes is a flagship boutique located along a fashionable downtown Fifth Avenue shopping block. This design and distribution company has outlets in the United States and Europe. The project addressed the design of all interior spaces, fixtures, furniture and the storefront.

The architectonic strategy incorporates the fundamental characteristics of the product: color, layering of materials, and comments on the sculptural nature of shoes.

The narrow and deep interior space is flanked on both sides by shelves the plasticity of which confers to the vertical planes a hieroglyphic quality and display shoes in a dramatic setting. The incised cuts in the new wall surfaces allow the shelves to alternatively recede and protrude from this new skin. The folds and cuts in the ceiling plane reveal fragments of an urban archeology juxtaposed to the new mechanical system. This double spatial strategy draws the eye into the full depth of the store. Lighting and mirrors emphasize and reveal architectonic episodes and the layered space. The cash/wrap counter is lit internally and glows white. Beyond, on the store's back wall facing the entry, a rear-lit glass plane slowly changes color from top to bottom, attracting attention from the passers-by.

The play of dark shadows against the white background brings forth the plasticity and depth of the layered elements and allows attention to focus on the color of the shoes on display.

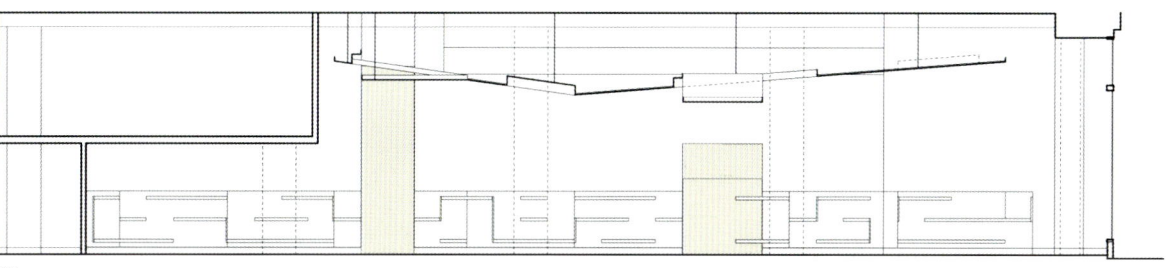

33.

STEPHEN ALTON / ARCHITECTURE: BODIES OF SPACE

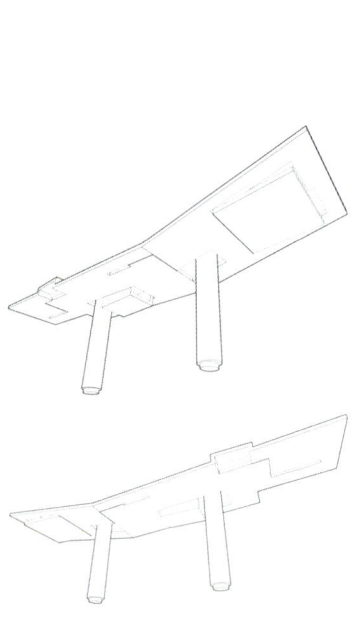

34. Mare Shoes. Floating ceiling, axonometric
35. Mare Shoes. Floating ceiling, axonometric
36. Mare Shoes. General view with floating ceiling

STEPHEN ALTON / ARCHITECTURE: BODIES OF SPACE

PROJECT **Donna Karan**

Donna Karan Beauty, Macy's, Herald Square, NYC
Bloomingdale's, NYC
Macy's, Fox Hills Mall, Culver City, CA
Macy's Union Square, San Francisco, CA
Liberty House, Ala Moana, HI

Harvey Nichols, London, England
Donna Karan Menswear, Jeddah, Saudi Arabia
DKNY/Donna Karan Collection, Al Amoudi, Saudi Arabia
Donna Karan Intimates, Macy's, Herald Square, NYC
Macy's Beverly Center, Los Angeles CA

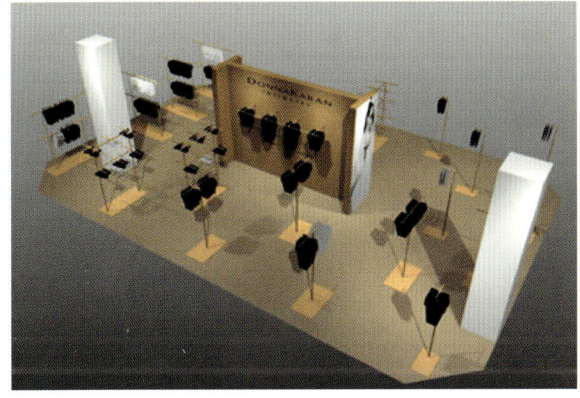

37.

The enormous success and widespread visibility of *Donna Karan Company* is due to a great product marketed through a brilliant use of advertising and design.

Stephen Alton has developed and detailed many projects for Donna Karan. Their success was due in great part to the close relationship that was formed with the *Creative Services Group* at *DK*. *Donna Karan Company* caused quite a stir when it introduced its new beauty line without licensing the product until much later on. *Stephen Alton Architect, P.C.*, worked closely with the marketing, display, packaging, and all the creative services required to launch the prototype for the new product and to design some of the first display units, just as Donna Karan was about to start her *DK Home* line.

In the work developed for *DK Intimates*, the particular challenge involved an effort to accommodate *DK*'s "look" and the requirements of the licensing company. The design developed prototype studies and flexible-while-elegant fixture units.

The *DK Collection* and *DKNY Men's Store* in Saudi Arabia was the first store to combine two separate lines in one hybrid design proposal. The conservative Saudi cultural context prohibits publicity for such non-traditional fashion.

37. Donna Karan Intimates. Prototype store, axonometric
38. Donna Karan Beauty. Counter prototype for Bloomingdales, in wood, bronze, back lit glass

38.

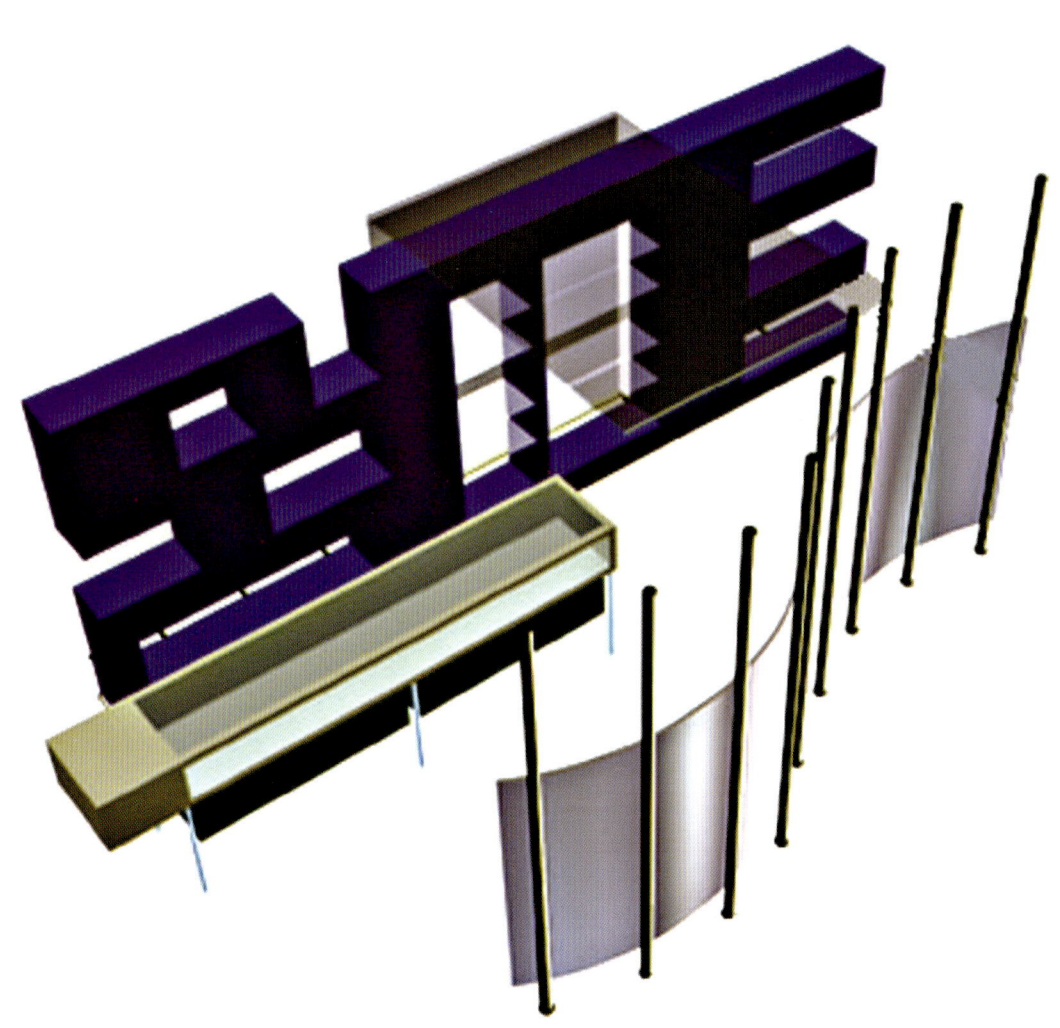

STEPHEN ALTON / ARCHITECTURE: BODIES OF SPACE

PROJECT **Royale Cards and Gifts**
177 West 4th Street, New York City

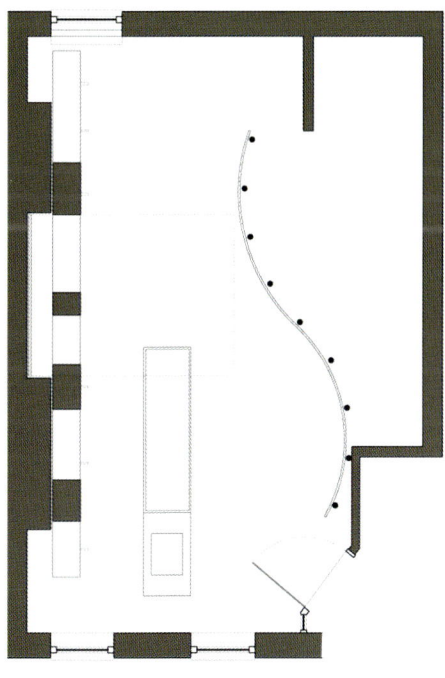

This award-winning small shop is dedicated mainly to postcards. The card wall is a fluid and transparent one, while the gift wall is solid and punctured. The materials employed are basic, and the project benefits from a simple installation. The card wall involves a perforated metal surface screwed to photographer's auto poles. The card holders are made of bent wire to fit the perforations. The curved, perforated metal surface goes from pole to pole and adds a sense of space and depth to this small store. The wire card holders form a versatile display system that can be reconfigured at will by the owner. The gift wall is built of painted plywood. The counter display is built with speed rail and plywood.

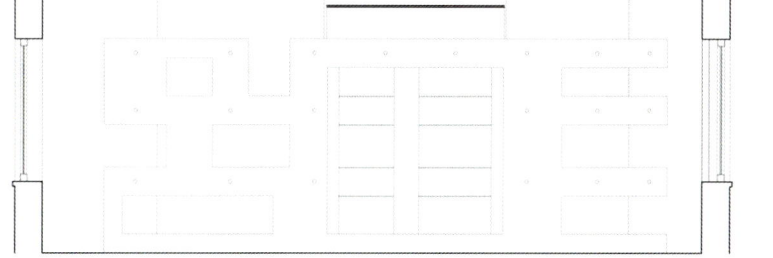

41.

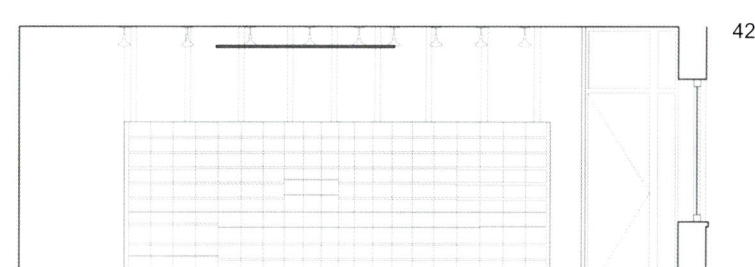

42.

43.

39. Royale Cards and Gifts. Project axonometric, previous pp 26
40. Royale Cards and Gifts. Plan
41. Royale Cards and Gifts. Elevation, gift display in plywood
42. Royale Cards and Gifts. Elevation, card display wall, autopoles and perforated metal
43. Royale Cards and Gifts. Gift display

44. Royale Cards and Gifts. Gift wall, painted plywood, glass, and speed rail
45. Royale Cards and Gifts. Card wall, autopoles, perforated metal, bent wire

PROJECT **Sacco Shoes**
Seventh Avenue, New York City

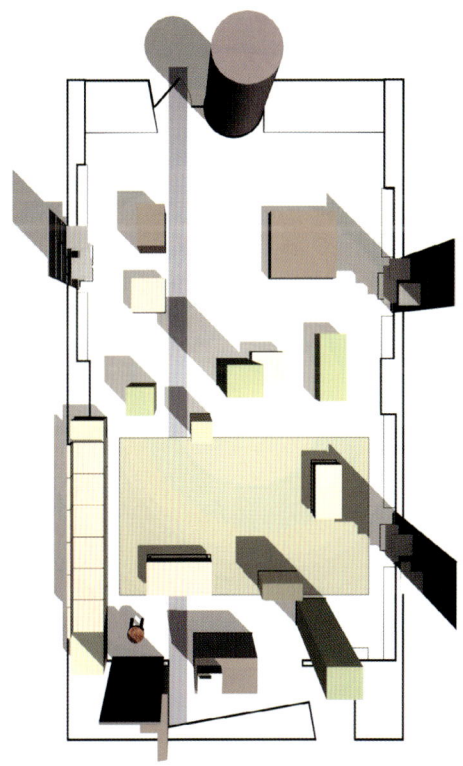

Often the strict budgetary and spatial parameters involved in smaller projects stimulate innovative design solutions. *Sacco* and *Royale* stores are good examples. A simple and careful use of materials produced low-tech and versatile systems for displaying merchandise. The store-planning projects for *Sacco* focused on redesigning the "found" retail spaces so that the modern image of this shoe company would keep pace with the character of its shoes. The versatility and endless design possibilities of "nomadic" installation and display units were employed to achieve "mobile" podiums, seating, and fixturing systems. Flexibility became the fundamental organizing instrument that governed the design of an environment where form and function blend harmoniously. This strategy allows effortless transitions to take place among seasonal merchandise lines.

46. Sacco Shoes. Plan
47. Sacco Shoes. View from the entry, tinted concrete floor and custom bench

STEPHEN ALTON / ARCHITECTURE: BODIES OF SPACE

49.

50.

48. Sacco Shoes. Sales area with custom made benches
49. Sacco Shoes. Display area with custom metal system for hanging bags
50. Sacco Shoes. View across store

48.

STEPHEN ALTON / ARCHITECTURE: BODIES OF SPACE 31

PROJECT **Ligne Roset**
Post Road, Westport, Connecticut

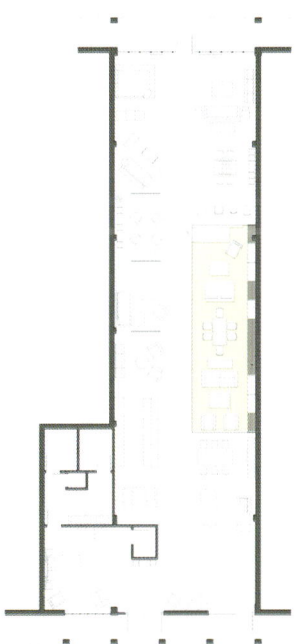

The *Ligne Roset* glass-front facade forms a proscenium that heralds the store beyond for car drivers, passengers, and pedestrians alike at this busy intersection in Westport. Suspended plastic colored panels act as a scrim in a theatrical composition that tints the interior space and furniture, and thus emphasizes the numerous color and fabric choices available. A yellow chair may sequentially appear orange, then red, or both colors as viewed through the facade.

The ceiling steps down from the revealed steel trusses at the street frontage to the ceiling at the rear. Groups of furniture and the control of the perceptual depth of the store are organized by ceiling and floor-height variations, by lighting and materials.

Accessories are displayed in the solid mass of cabinetry and its carved-out shelves, contrasting with the thin "skins" of the facade's glass and plastic panels, in a composition coordinated by color, light, and geometry.

The white walls and ceilings allow for the facade and cabinetry alone to provide vibrant saturated color accents that complement the palette of *Ligne Roset*'s furniture. The color effects can be changed easily by replacing the plastic panels, switching the removable translucent display-wall panels, or by repainting the interiors of the carved-out shelves. This flexibility leaves room for the next year's furniture palette. This store prototype anticipates other, future showcases for *Ligne Roset* furniture.

51. Ligne Roset. Floor plan
52. Ligne Roset. Entry view with color panels
53. Ligne Roset. Interior view and display wall, with epoxy resin floor, following pp 32

PROJECTS   **Private Residences**

Apartment 22
Apartment 11
Loft: Dual Space / Seidmon Residence
House Addition: Art Port / Krug andHaubrich
Other Interiors

STEPHEN ALTON / ARCHITECTURE: BODIES OF SPACE

PROJECT   **Apartment 22**
New York City

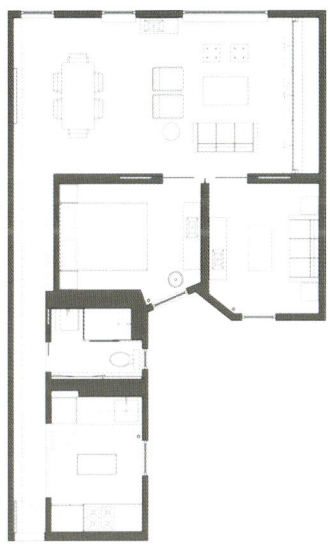

This medium-size apartment for Dlutowski and Occolowitz is located one floor above *Apartment 11* at the same address.

The project involves a series of planes that slip into wall surfaces and forms a pink translucent layer. This occurs at the bathroom and at the bedroom doors. A slot in the bathroom door had a special film applied that allows for clear vision on angles but no image when looking straight ahead. This voyeuristic door element was also explored in the treatment of the shower stall and the pivoting, faceted mirrors in the bathroom. The bathroom has a custom-poured epoxy sink, lighted from the floor, that slips into the mirrored wall. The surfaces of the hidden storage in the living room appear as floating white planes, each ot them having a different directional and surface angle, and leading to an aleatoric compositional effect. This surface treatment was elaborated in *Atlas* with mirrored panels. The sliding doors in the living room lead to the bedrooms and bathroom. The all-white kitchen contrasts with the all-black one in *Apartment 11*. The lighting throughout the apartment washes the wall surfaces that have either moving elements below, such as cabinet doors, and/or faceted surfaces that allow shadows to participate in emphasizing the quality of the surface finishes.

56. Apartment 22. Living room storage wall, pp 33
57. Apartment 22. Concept view at bathroom, with sliding door panels, previous pp 34
58. Apartment 22. Plan
59. Apartment 22. Concept section through gallery

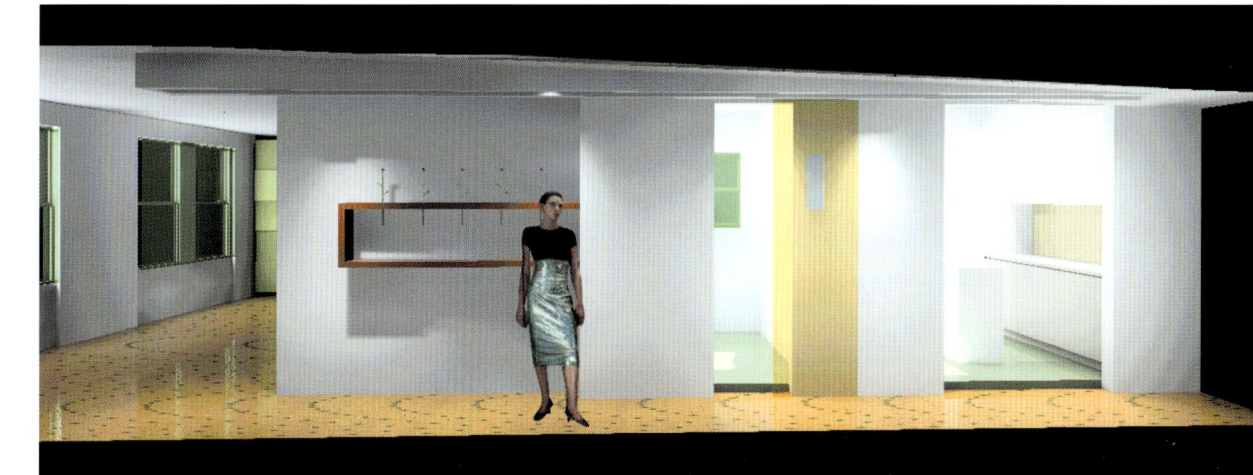

36   STEPHEN ALTON / ARCHITECTURE: BODIES OF SPACE

58.

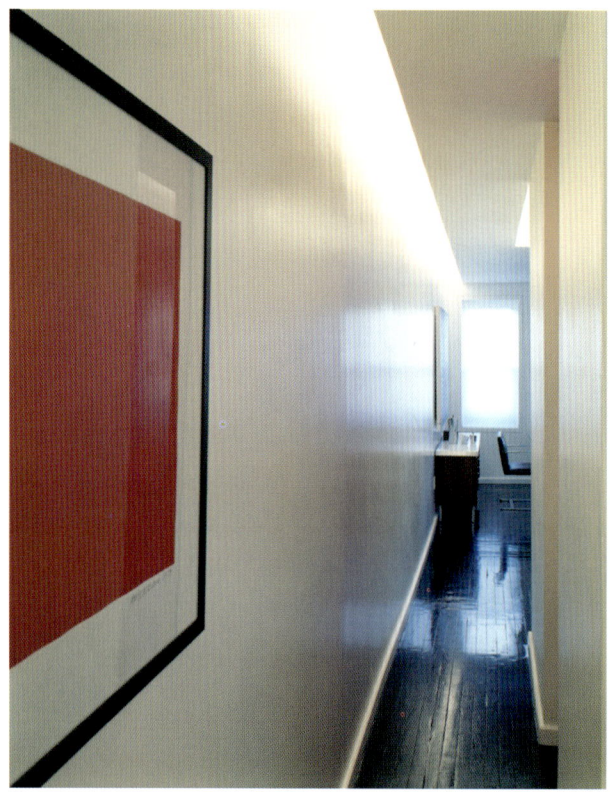

59.

60.

58. Apartment 22. Ceiling at entry
59. Apartment 22. Entry/Gallery
60. Apartment 22. Bedroom entry with color laminated pocket door and faceted glass medicine cabinet
61. Apartment 22. Kitchen with painted wood cabinets, stainless steel appliances, sand blasted mirror backsplash, and Corian tops
62. Apartment 22. Kitchen
63. Apartment 22. Living and dining area, with color interlaminate door to bedrooms, tinted hardwood floors, pp 37

61.

62.

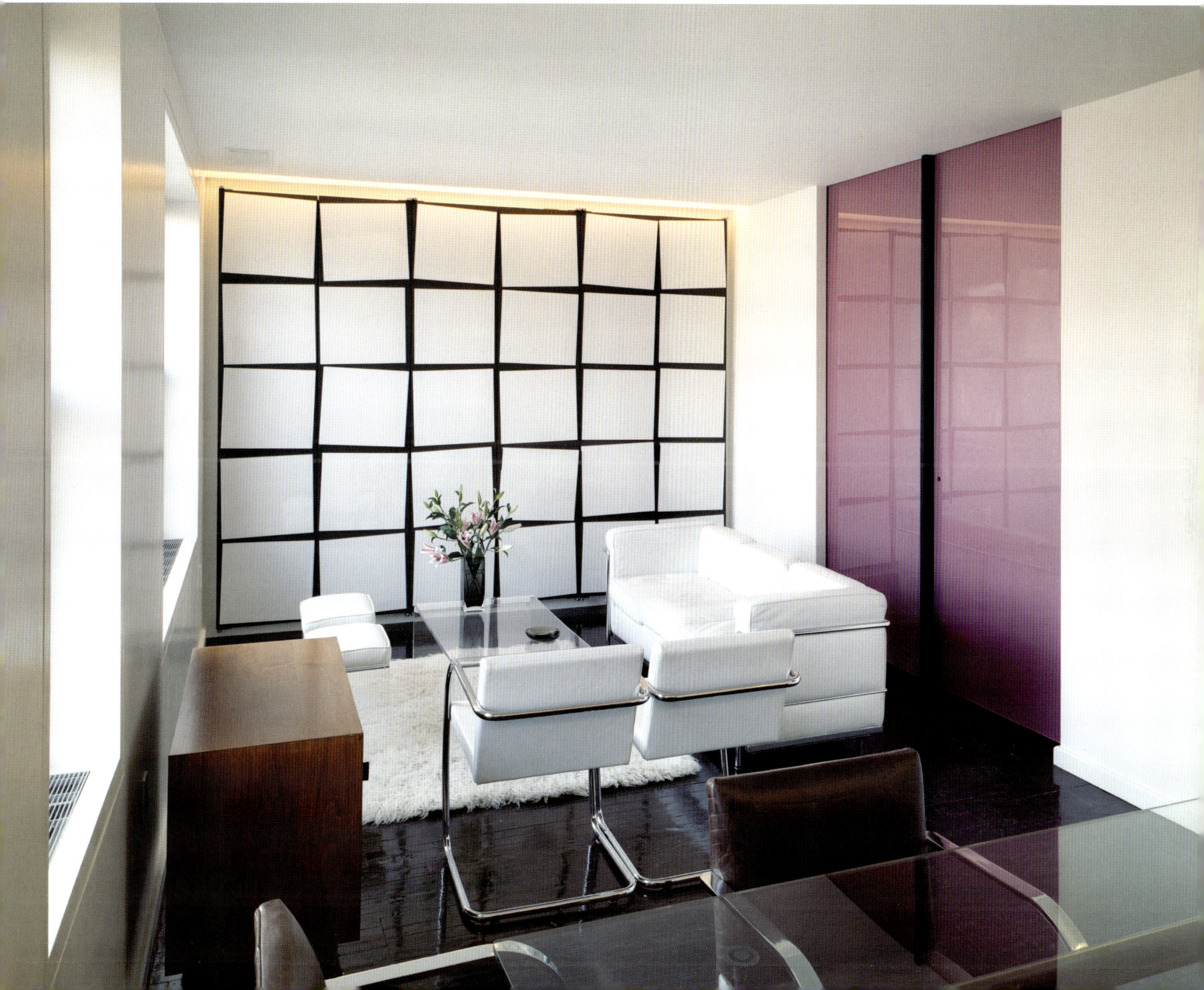

STEPHEN ALTON / ARCHITECTURE: BODIES OF SPACE

64. Apartment 22. Bathroom detail, custom poured epoxy sink, mirrored wall with medicine cabinet behind, colored interlayer glass shower enclosure

PROJECT Apartment 11
New York City

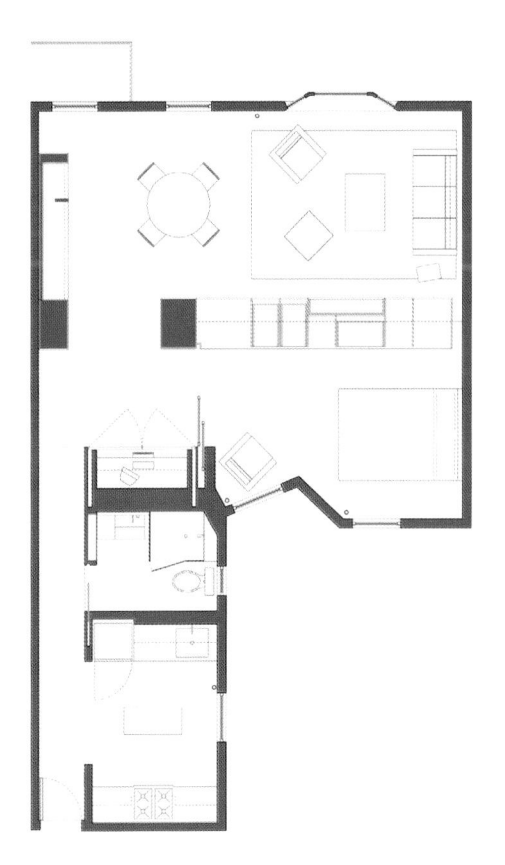

This medium-size apartment is located in the Chelsea neighborhood of New York. The apartment is located one floor below *Apartment 22*, as a variation on its theme. The construction included reconfiguring the bedroom areas and redesign of all areas of the apartment.

The project was conceived as an existing envelope, with insertions of bath/kitchen areas of waxed- concrete surfacing and the open areas of the living room/bedroom to be separated by a "mobile." The storage for the TV/stereo cabinet is a freestanding solid volume detailed in tinted, limed quarter-sawn oak that is disengaged spatially by the glassed space above and to the sides, and by sliding glass doors that allow for privacy. It separates the living room area from the bedroom. The solid volume of the bath/kitchen area acts as an engaged poché rather than being free-floating as in *Apartment 22*. A clear change of envelope to filled-in poché occurs at the floor to the kitchen and hallway. The concrete kitchen floor is raised above the wood floor, as revealed at the connection with the corresponding opening. The kitchen has soapstone counters. A custom bookshelf covered in linen is located in the living area. A built-in office is behind doors off the dining area. Careful attention was paid to paint colors throughout.

65. Apartment 11. Plan

66. Apartment 11. View from the living room towards the master bedroom, sliding metal door, pickled oak storage

67. Apartment 11. View from the seating area towards dining, pickled oak storage cabinet, linen-wrapped bookshelf, stained mahogany floors

STEPHEN ALTON / ARCHITECTURE: BODIES OF SPACE

68.

69.

70.

71.

68. Apartment 11. Bathroom, waxed concrete walls, sliding glass pocket door
69. Apartment 11. Bathroom, sliding glass and metal door, pickled oak storage
70. Apartment 11. View of the gallery and kitchen areas
71. Apartment 11. Kitchen, soap stone counter and inset sink, stained wood cabinets, waxed concrete floors

STEPHEN ALTON / ARCHITECTURE: BODIES OF SPACE

72. Apartment 11. Bathroom, concrete walls and floor, light slot, sink of stainless steel and fruitwood, removable wood slat at shower floor

STEPHEN ALTON / ARCHITECTURE: BODIES OF SPACE 43

PROJECT **Seidmon Residence**
Greenwich Village, New York City

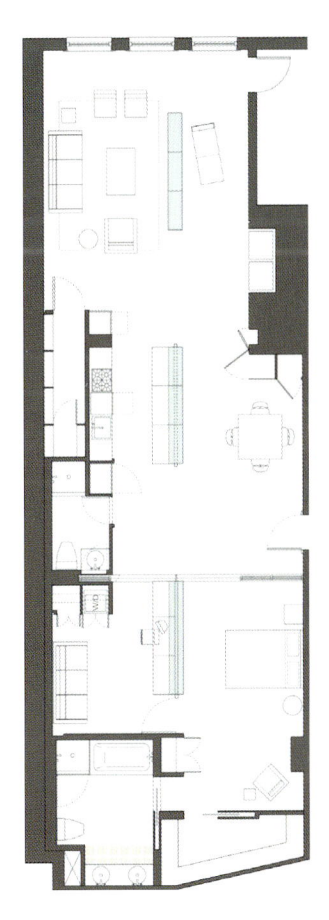

This medium size Manhattan residential loft was configured and detailed so as to allow for privacy while preserving the sense of a large open loft. Sliding glass and steel doors with clear upper panes and translucent lower panes ennable light to reach the rear of the loft and still provide privacy. The architectural elements of the apartment were developed as "furniture." Materials were used to articulate the different parts of the design program, and each element was detailed to read as an object that does not touch the perimeter walls or ceiling. This is similar to the way "furniture" sits in an interior space.

The plan of the apartment was developed to allow the limited natural light of the living and kitchen areas at the norhtern front end of the apartment to reach the bedroom and study at the rear of the loft. This literal transparancy was accomplished by a custom sliding metal and glass screen running on an east/west axis. A north/south division was deliniated by cabinetry units that form a partition wall. These units involve cantelevered work surfaces made of industrial lab top materials held by custom metal supports. The tops are attached to an industrial plastic resin coated "finply" base unit, a plywood material that is typically used for concrete formwork. Clearstory windows at walls and upper panels of the sliding screen produce the effect a continuous ceiling plane. The large volume clad in Anagre wood paneling contains the kitchen/powder room/laundry "furniture." This singular, large solid volume, helps to organize the "wet" functional requirements. The design elements for this apartment involve one object, one transparent plane, and one furniture wall that organizes the programmatic and functional requirements. Other materials used involved waxed plaster wall surface finishes on the "wet" wall, custom lighting elements, and custom stainless doorpulls.

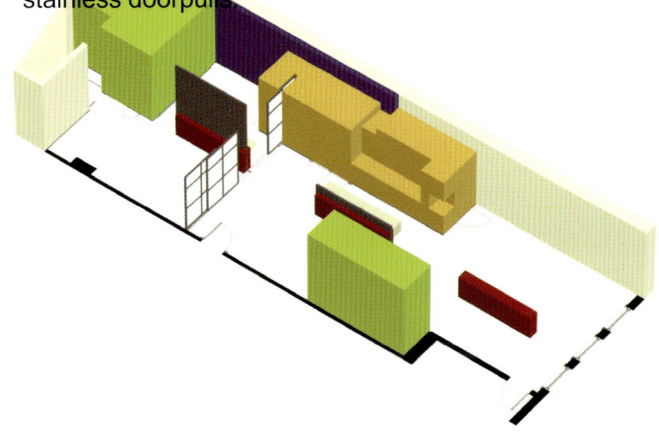

73. Seidmon Residence. Plan
74. Seidmon Residence. Axonometric

75. Seidmon Residence. Detail at kitchen and bathroom, steel and glass doors, anagre wood
76. Seidmon Residence. Steel and glass doors, anagre wood at kitchen and bathroom volume, lab top counters, special Belgian plywood coated red
77. Seidmon Residence. Industrial formwork, red plywood, metal and glass doors clerestory
78. Seidmon Residence. Kitchen and dining
79. Seidmon Residence. Kitchen and dining
80. Seidmon Residence. Detail at kitchen counter, lab top counters, stainless steel and blackened steel structure for counters, glass

STEPHEN ALTON / ARCHITECTURE: BODIES OF SPACE 45

80.

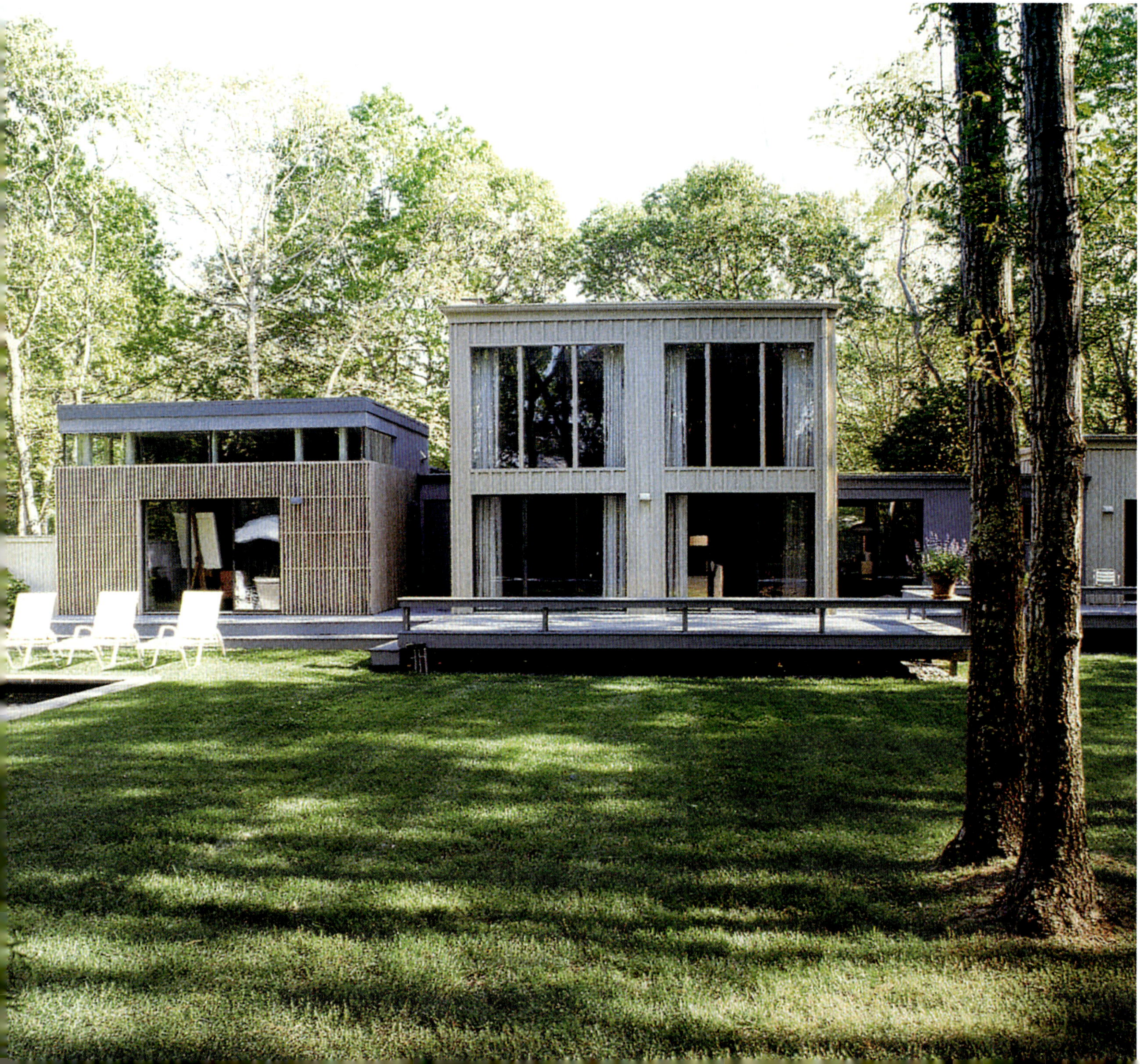

PROJECT   **Art Port: Krug and Haubrich Residence**
East Hampton, Long Island, New York

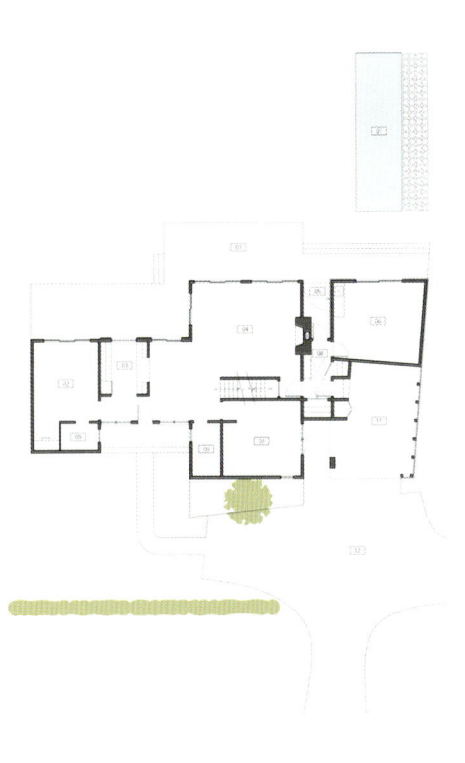

The original and rather boxy house was built in the 1970s. It is typical of the area, with wood-frame construction and large windows facing the rear. The scope of work involved the addition of a car port and an art port/ artist studio, storage, and mud room, redesign of the entry areas, changes to the driveway, and landscaping.

The addition balances the masses of the carport and art port around a large central volume. The formal intention was to pull apart the vertical wood facing of exterior skin of the building and establish a tension between the old and the new skins, between the port for cars and the port for making art, alluding to the stretching of canvas over a frame.

The interior employs raw materials such as homosote. This bespeaks of a working painting studio. It allows for the pinning of various objects to the wall. The exterior surface was conceived of and layered to produce a solid gray box endowed with a transparent skin that wraps it and reveals the solid underlying building made of concrete board that is usually coated with stucco. The material was left raw and with exposed connectors. The wooden skin was wrapped around the solid understructure and it forms a translucent barrier that surrounds the carport and then continues around the studio. The clerestory window and north window are on an axis with the pool. The scale of the single sliding "north window" is proportionately related to the existing sliders of the main house. This door is slightly disengaged from the exterior surface. The definition of "finished" is placed into question in response to some of the program components: a place for painting and a place for shading a car. The function determines the finish.

81. Krug and Haubrich Residence. Arrival to Art Port, pp 46
82. Krug and Haubrich Residence. Art Port plan

48 STEPHEN ALTON / ARCHITECTURE: BODIES OF SPACE

83.

84.

85.

83. Krug and Haubrich Residence. View at front of house
84. Krug and Haubrich Residence. View at rear of house
85. Krug and Haubrich Residence. View along side of Art Port, wood slate over concrete volume
86. Krug and Haubrich Residence. Elevation at rear of house
87. Krug and Haubrich Residence. Interior of artis studio, homosote walls and painted wood trim, lanseal floors
88. Krug and Haubrich Residence. Detail at clerestory window
89. Krug and Haubrich Residence. Elevation at side of Art Port
90. Krug and Haubrich Residence. Elevation at rear of house

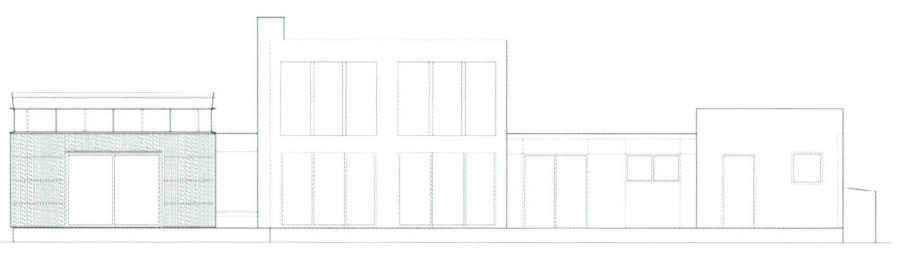

86.

STEPHEN ALTON / ARCHITECTURE: BODIES OF SPACE

87.  88.

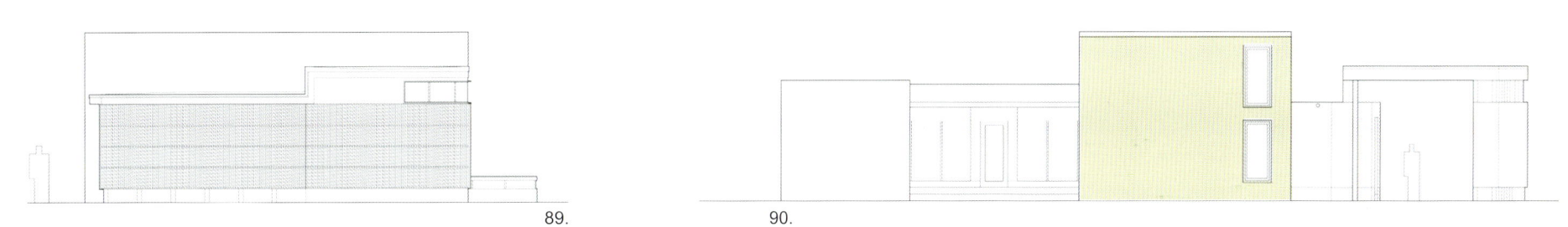

89. 90.

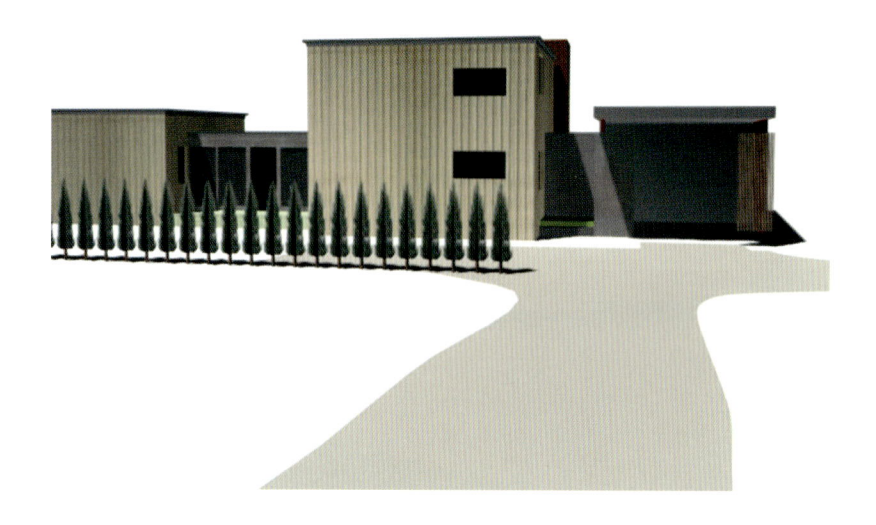

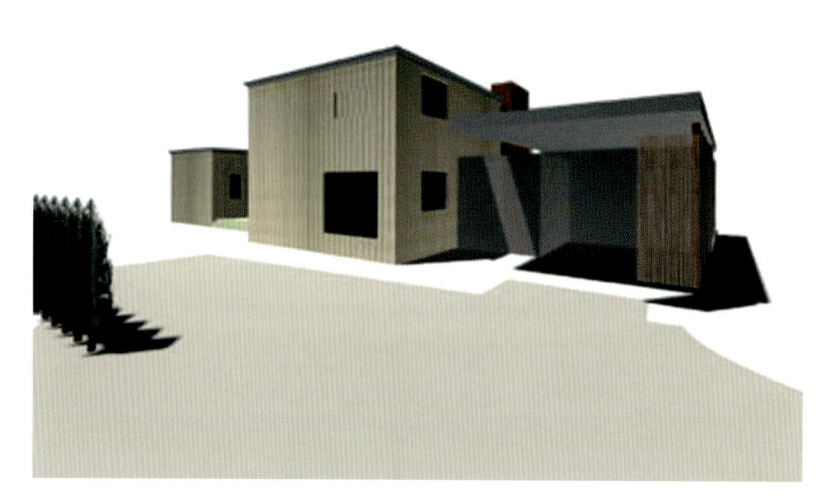

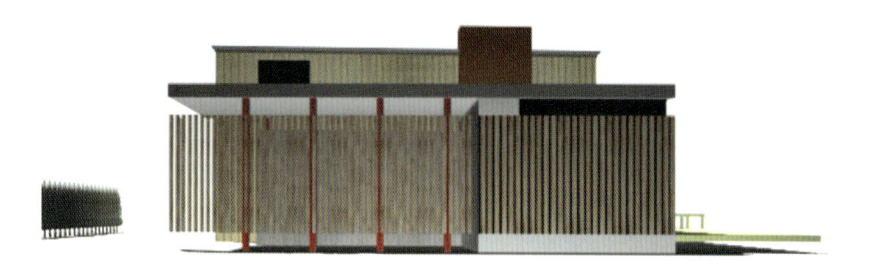

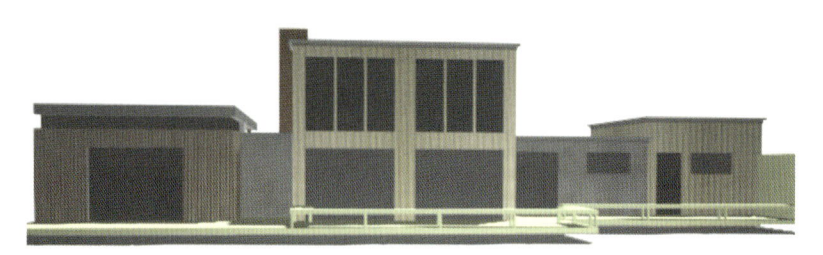

91. Krug and Haubrich Residence. View of entry from the street
92. Krug and Haubrich Residence. Approach to Art Port
93. Krug and Haubrich Residence. Side view of Art Port, wood slat skin with concrete volume beneath
94. Krug and Haubrich Residence. Rear view of the house with Art Port on the left

STEPHEN ALTON / ARCHITECTURE: BODIES OF SPACE 51

PROJECTS   **Other Residences**
New York City

 95. Office
 96. Office
 97. Residence. Kitchen
 99. Residence. Kitchen, living room
100. Residence. Living room
101. Residence. Living room

103. Apartment. Living room
104. Apartment. Study area
105. Apartment. Living room
106. Apartment. Living room
107. Apartment. Studio bedroom
108. Apartment. Bedroom
109. Apartment. Sitting/dining area
110. Apartment. Bathroom
111. Apartment. Bedroom

PROJECTS   Housing and Other Studies

Concept Restaurant
Astor
The Hudson Tea Building "A"
Hotel Villa La Angostura

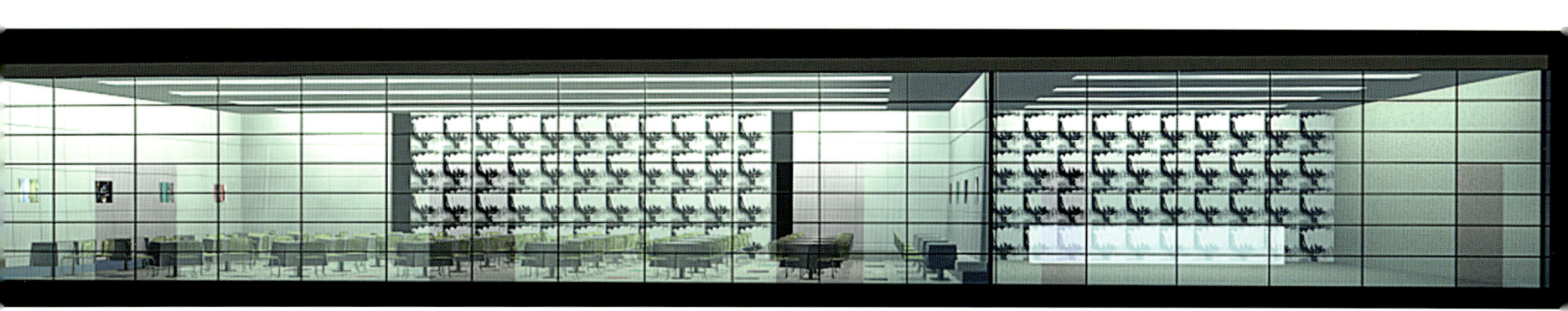

STEPHEN ALTON / ARCHITECTURE: BODIES OF SPACE

112. Concept Restaurant. Elevation at film wall to restaurant in the bar areas framing views for urban voyeurs, previous pp 53
113. Concept Restaurant. View of the dining room area with monitors in walls and floors

STEPHEN ALTON / ARCHITECTURE: BODIES OF SPACE

PROJECT **Concept Restaurant**
Study for *Planet Holywood*

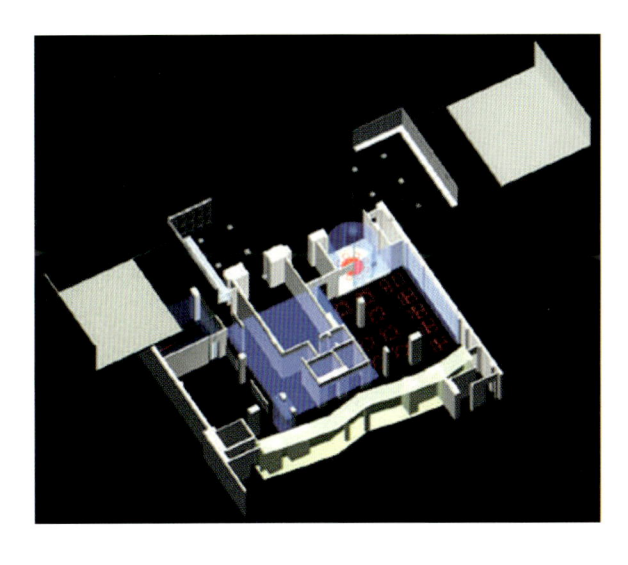

This prototype restaurant for a national chain was conceived so that the primary programmatic elements can be configured flexibly, depending on the site conditions. The program includes a large waiting hall, bar, dining, possible private dining room, with rear kitchen and service areas. Functional adjacencies and the use of materials produce a stagelike atmosphere and cinematic sequence related to the owner's brand.

The dividing surface between the waiting area and the bar/dining areas was broken into frames, and a unique new material involving glass filament laminated in glass, allowing for a clear view only when looking straight ahead and a blurred view if looking on angle to the surface of the glass, was incorporated to enhance the voyeuristic and film quality of the spaces. The visitors can watch and in turn can be watched. Alongside the waiting area there is a large Rauschenberg-like box filled with film-star paraphernalia and reflecting back the opposing framed surface brings a surreal quality to the event. Video cameras project images of people caught in the between spaces, and motors were placed in all surfaces including floors and walls. Floors and walls are saturated with video screens continuously playing movies.

The walls behind the restaurant and the bar are backlighted in repeated floral patterns as an homage to Warhol and alluding to techniques of film editing. The flower images involve photos by Karl Blossfeldt, the German naturalist and photographer credited with introducing images from the scientific world as art.

114. Concept Restaurant. Axonometric
115. Concept Restaurant. View of the waiting corridor with "Rauschenberg" box on the left, and film wall on the right

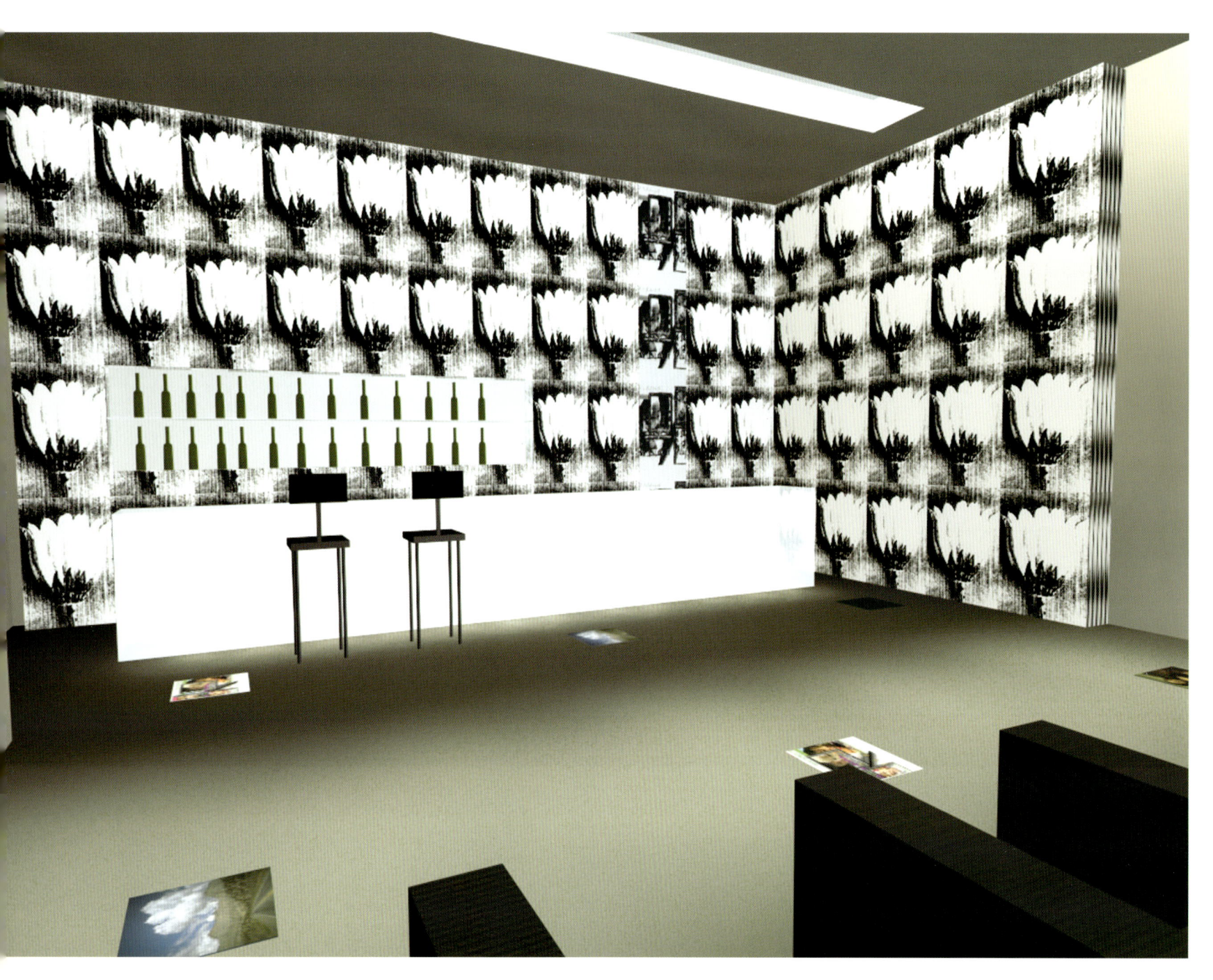

116. Concept Restaurant. Bar with back lighted
    Karl Blossfeldt pop art wall and light box bar

STEPHEN ALTON / ARCHITECTURE: BODIES OF SPACE 57

PROJECT **Astor**
Astor Place, New York City

This residential apartment building lobby involves a design for public space. The site condition led to the angular approach to the interior design of the lobby, circulation, and the sequence of internal space events.

This study anticipates the approach that was later developed in the *Atlas*. The intention of the design was to fragment systematically all of the surfaces, by either separation, warping, or cutouts, so that each architectonic element reaches its own state of autonomy. The slotted ceiling plane is floated apart from the walls that act as devices to warp space as initially formed by planar surfaces. The materials are engaged sectionally and determine the quality of the space, as in the corridor, where the soffit mimics the changes in floor finish and the color palette. The project is conceived as a porous body. The logic of light generates the geometry of the surface incisions and determines the character of elements like the elevator or the ceiling of the circulation spaces. The entry desk punctures glass. Materials are used as unadulterated solid elements, such as is the case with the single, frameless glass pane that separates the mail room from the lobby.

117. Astor. Lobby plan
118. Astor. Reflected ceiling plan

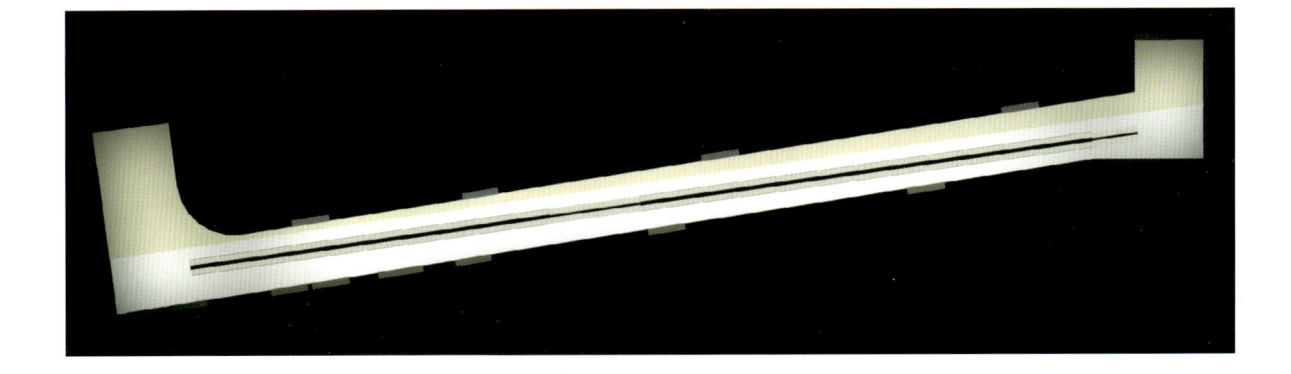

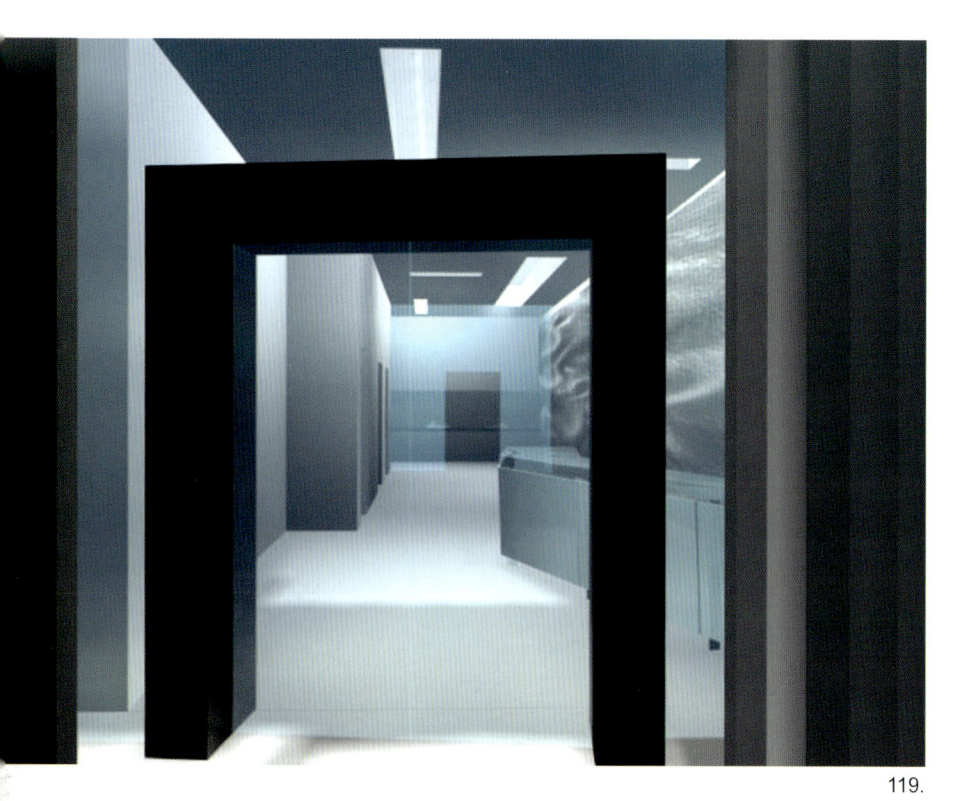

119. Astor. Entry vestibule with metal door frame and glass wall
120. Astor. View at corridor
121. Astor. Detail at desk penetration of glass wall at vestibule
122. Astor. View from mail area towards entry
123. Astor. View from entry at concierge metal and stone desk, stone floor, surfaces of specialty paint

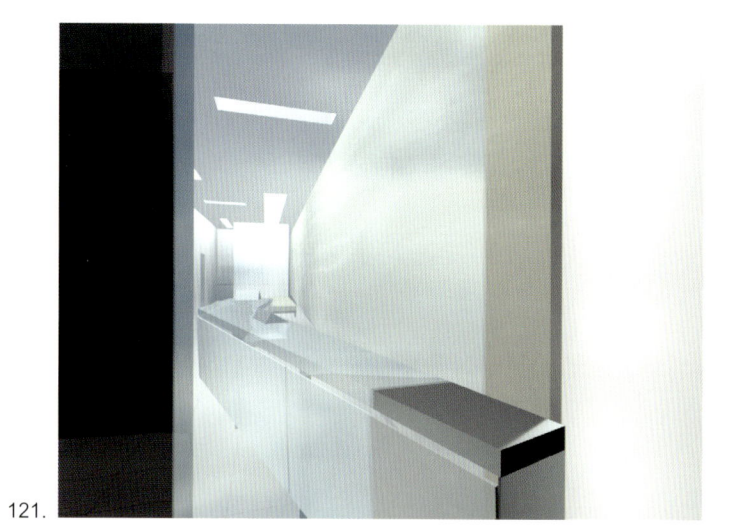

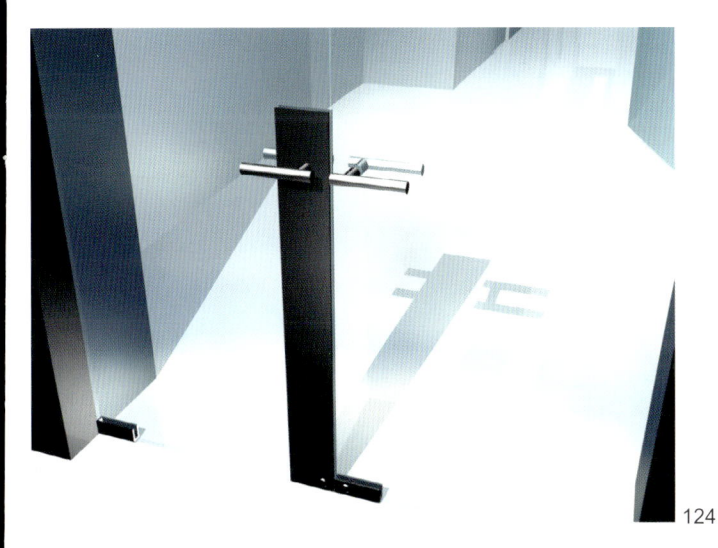

STEPHEN ALTON / ARCHITECTURE: BODIES OF SPACE

124. Astor. Door handle detail
125. Astor. Detail at typical ceiling corridor
126. Astor. Elevator, metal panels and inset glass light boxes

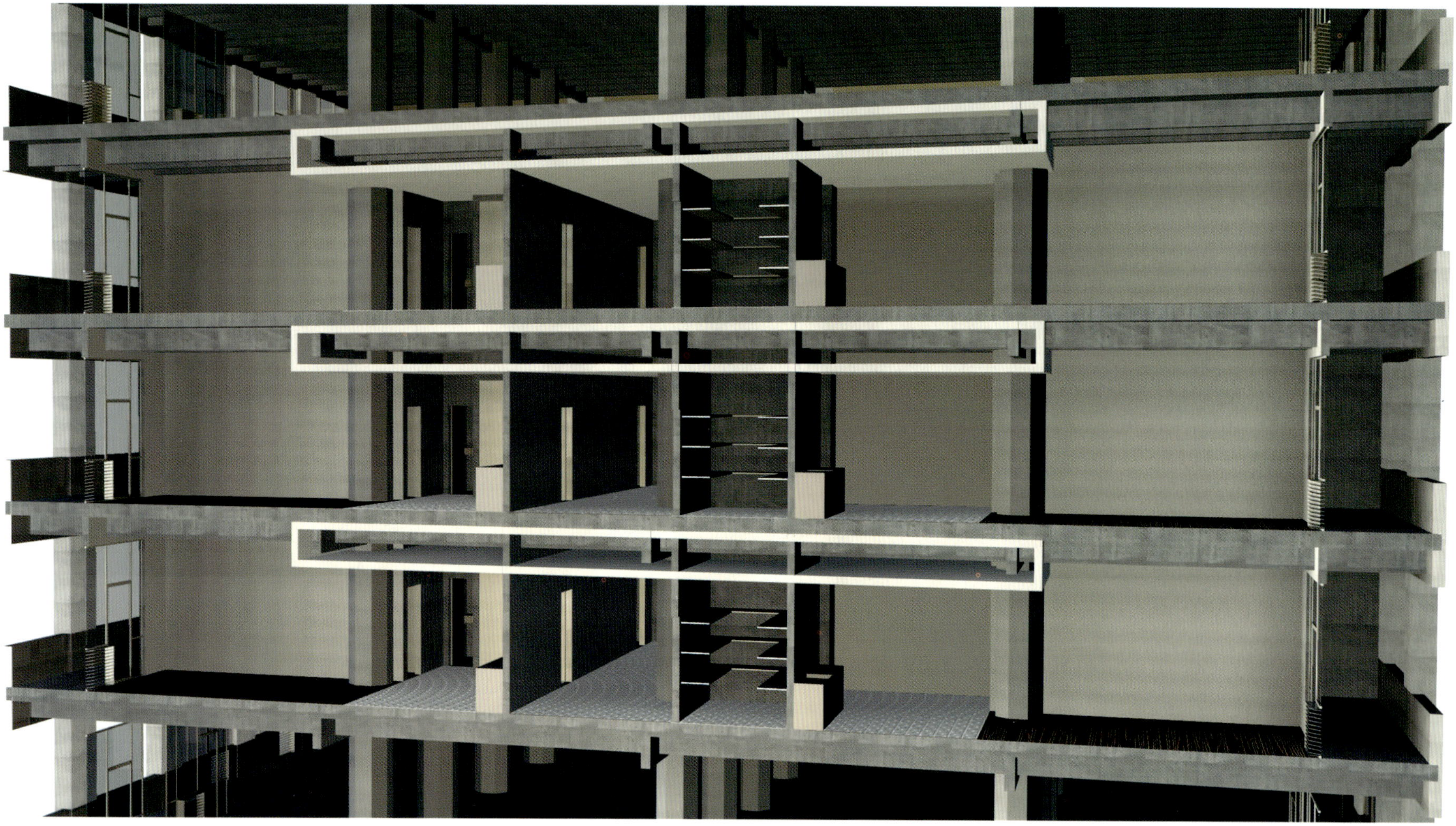

PROJECT **Hudson Tea White Building "A"**
Hoboken, New Jersey
Owners: CSFB

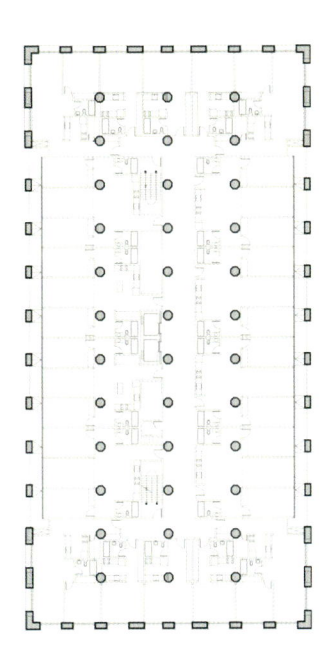

This 200-unit residential development was the former factory for the *Lipton Tea Co*. The existing concrete shell will be provided with a new facade and the respective mechanical systems. The dificulty posed by the floor-plate dimensions was resolved without "cutting" or demolishing the existing shell. This was a directive of the owner in response to zoning and cost parameters.

An "egg crate" facade on the east and west is a sunshade that helps maintain the unit depth to the acceptable 40 feet imposed by natural-light and air requirements and the proposed through-the-exterior-wall climate system. The facade setback offers unit-planning flexibility and it prevents the structural grid from dictating the position of the interior walls. A marketable loft-like quality for all of the interior spaces thus becomes achievable. The exterior is a combination of brick and stone. The new facade involves a precast system designed to be lifted into place and clipped to the existing structure.

The solution maximizes the use of floor area given the market value of typical-size units, and simultaneously provides rational unit depth. The pushed-back external skin and the storage area of the internal corridor reduce the initially problematic unit depth. This allows the required density to be achieved and provides for flexible layout. The building "skin" is the result of a unique combination of various events that dictates a hybrid solution.

127. Hudson Tea White Building "A."
Typical building section along east/west axis, previous pp 60
128. Hudson Tea White Building "A."
Typical plan
129. Hudson Tea White Building "A."
Site, aerial view

STEPHEN ALTON / ARCHITECTURE: BODIES OF SPACE

130. Hudson Tea White Building "A." Exterior rendering
131. Hudson Tea White Building "A." Exterior rendering from the center of the complex
132. Hudson Tea White Building "A." Program and massing studies
133. Hudson Tea White Building "A." Precast eggcrate detail section
134. Hudson Tea White Building "A." Axononometric of precast eggcrate and typical facade assembly
135. Hudson Tea White Building "A." Axonometric of typical two bedrooms unit, pp 63

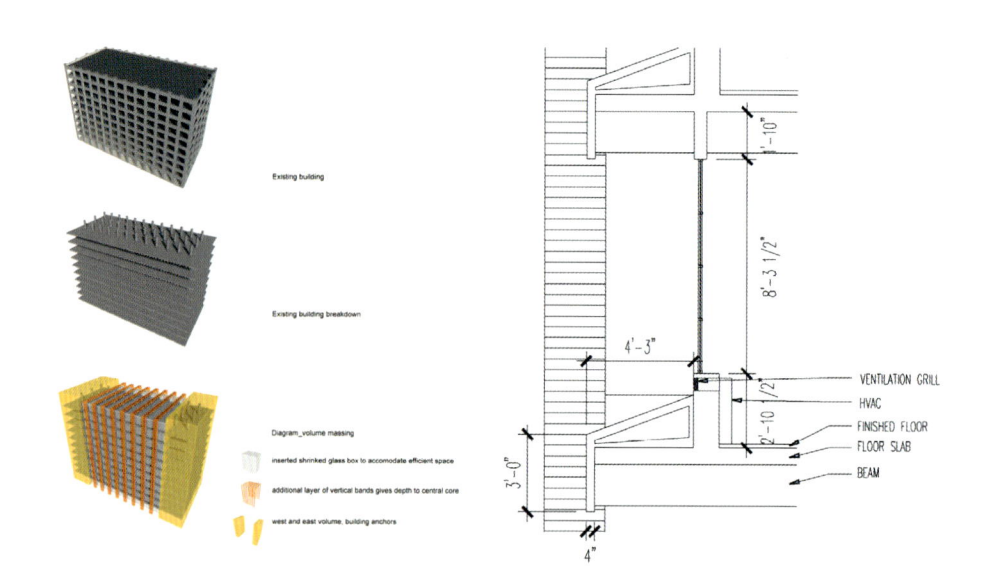

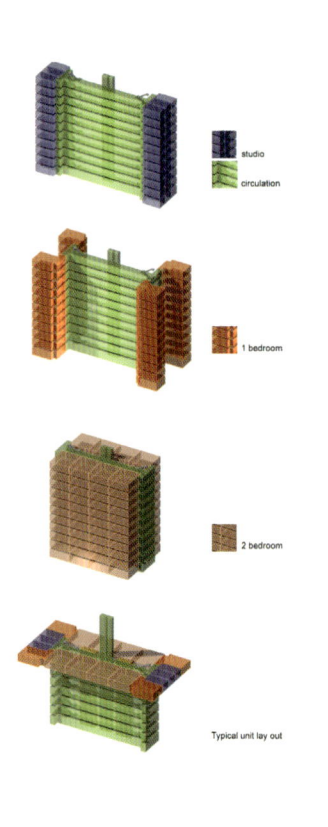

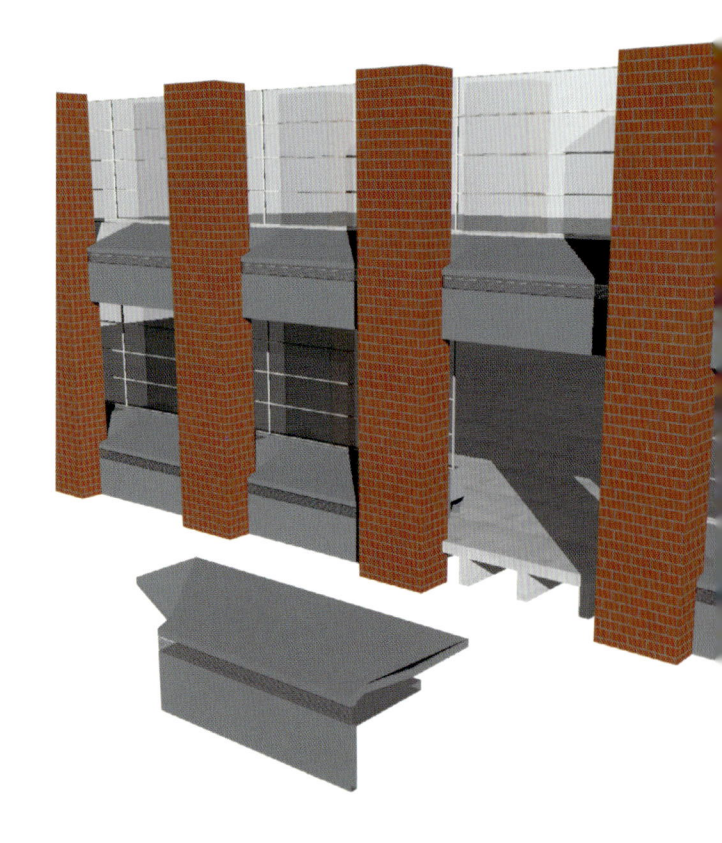

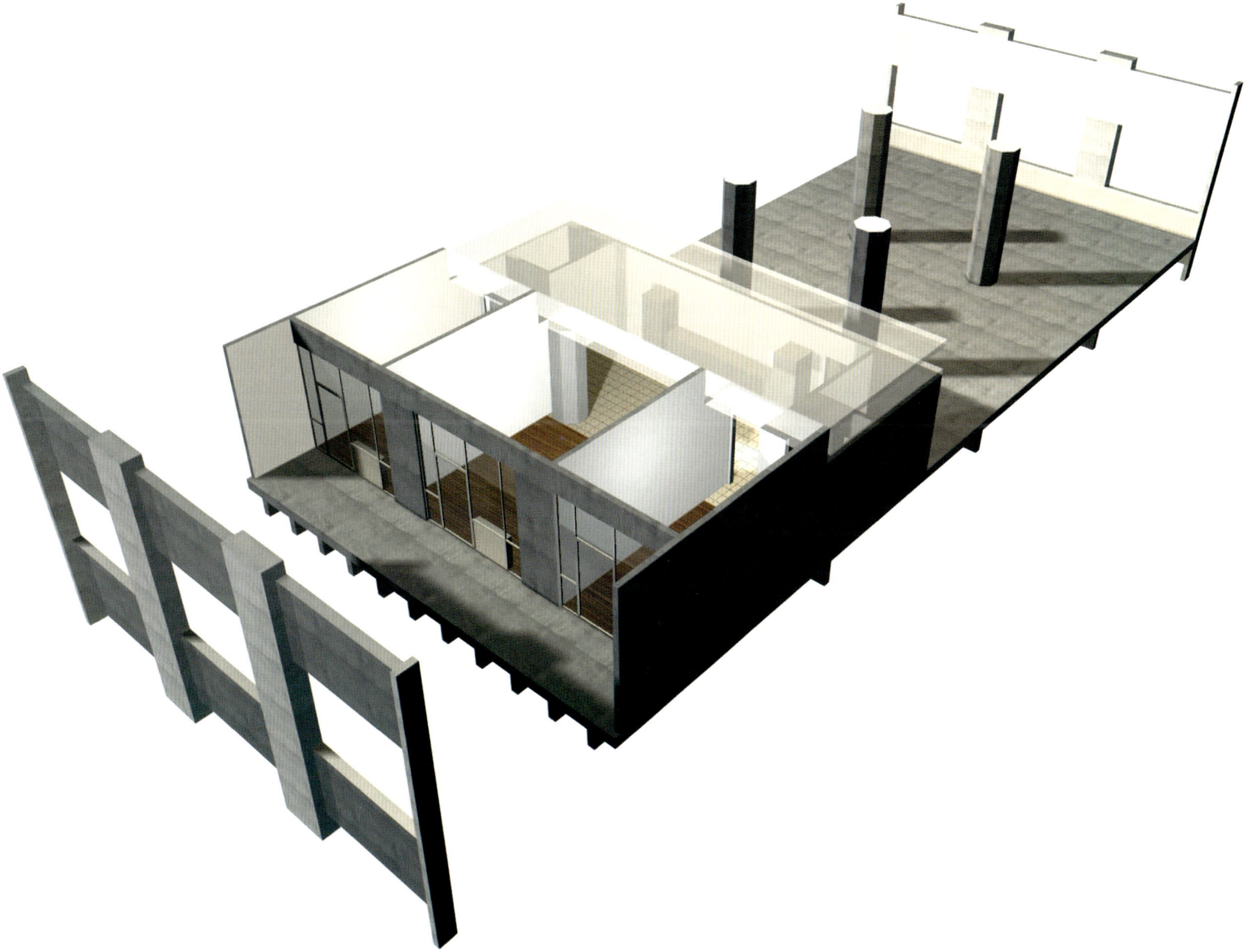

64 STEPHEN ALTON / ARCHITECTURE: BODIES OF SPACE

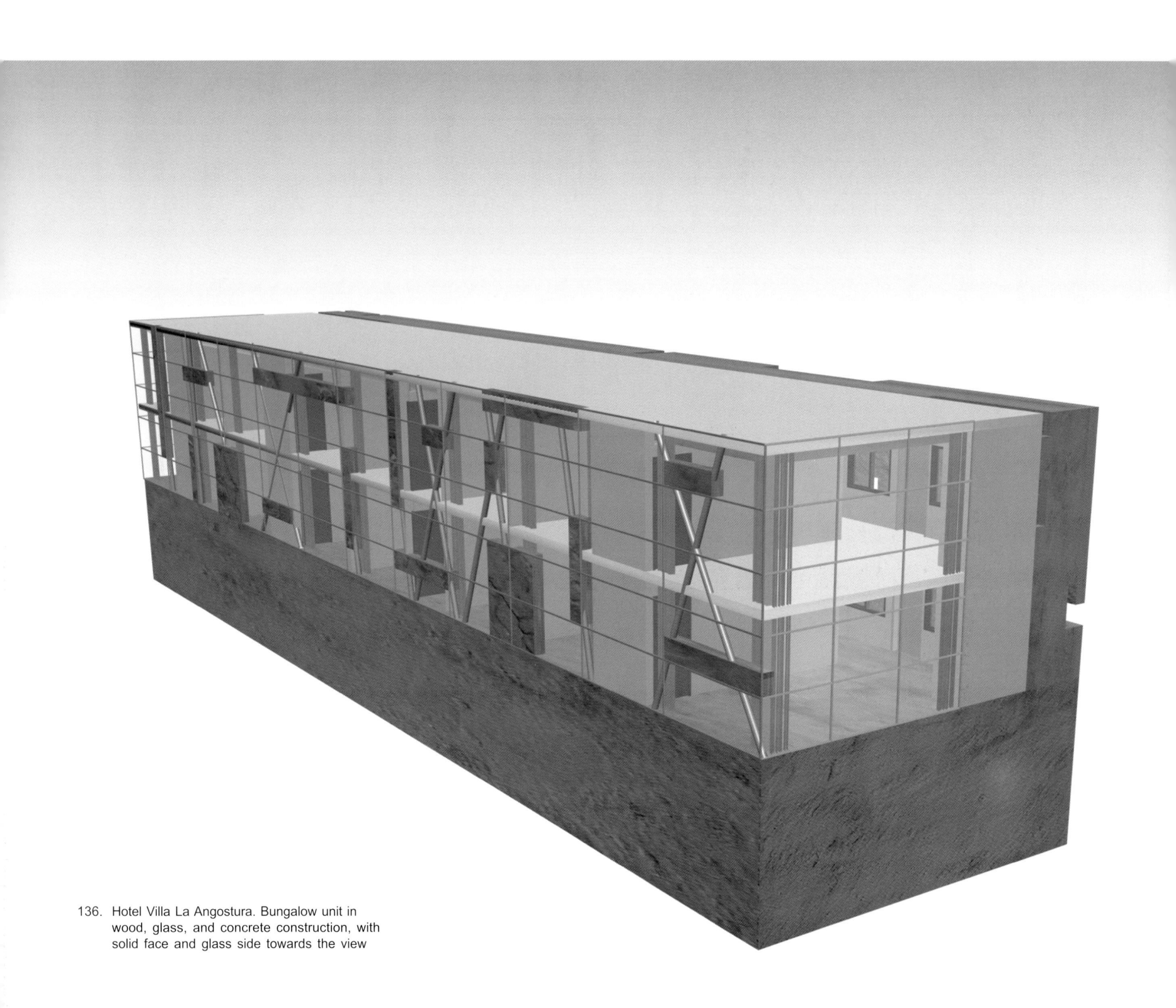

136. Hotel Villa La Angostura. Bungalow unit in wood, glass, and concrete construction, with solid face and glass side towards the view

STEPHEN ALTON / ARCHITECTURE: BODIES OF SPACE   65

PROJECT   **Hotel Villa La Angostura**
Nahuel Huapi National Park, Tierra del Fuego, Argentina

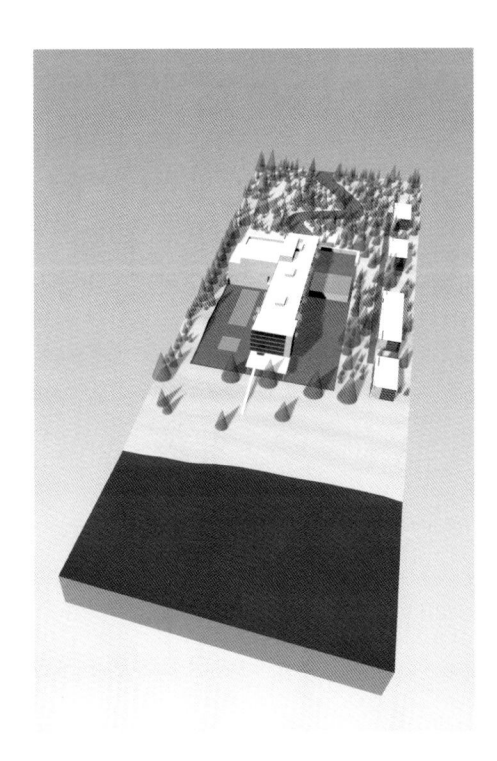

The hotel occupies a site in a densely forested national park, and slopes to a large lake. During the winter the area supports skiing nearby. In the summer the lake offers waterskiing and various other water-related activities. The program involves lobbies, a restaurant, activities rooms, guest rooms, and a gym. Views are excellent in all directions and taken advantage of fully though the orientation of the proposal for each and every room. The activities room and a large observation deck are at the water end of the "bar" building and benefit from the dramatic panoramic view of the lake. The exterior skin of the main building is marked by retractable shading devices that allow for economical summer shading. Private guest cabins are a very close walk from the main building. The cabins' architectonic skins along the eastern edge of the site become marked by the internal structural systems. Inspiration for forms was from piles of logs found in the woods and stacked in a splayed manner. The site access and foot paths through the site accentuate the natural slope and the views.

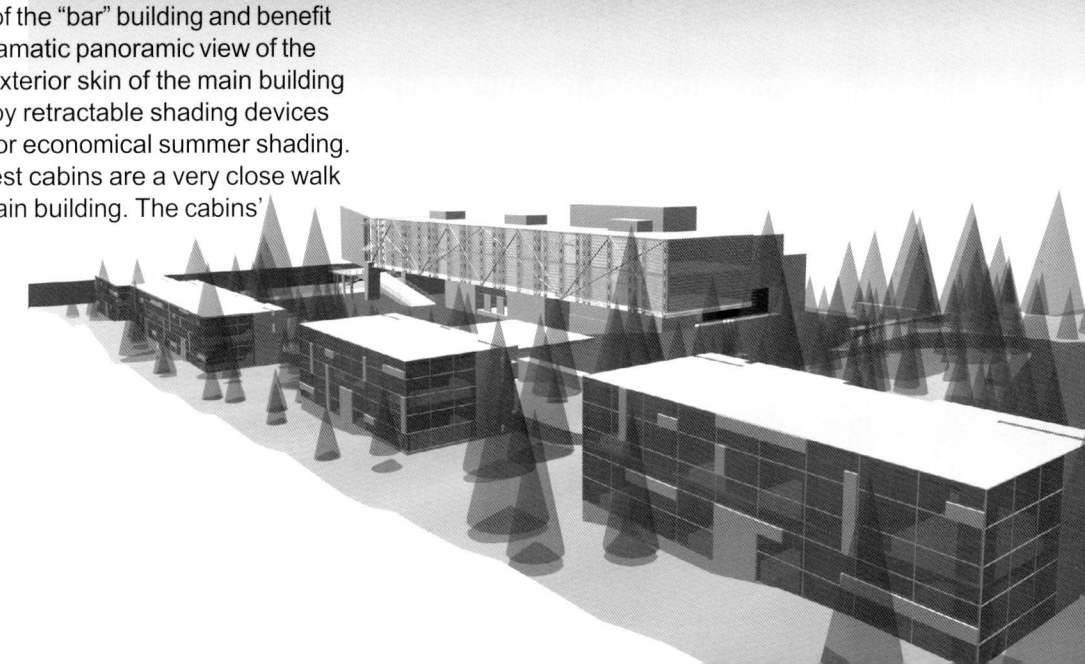

137. Hotel Villa La Angostura. Aerial site view with main building on the left, bungalows on the right, and lake in the foreground
138. Hotel Villa La Angostura. View of bungalows with main building in the background

66 STEPHEN ALTON / ARCHITECTURE: BODIES OF SPACE

139. Hotel La Angostura. View at drive up entry drop off point
140. Hotel La Angostura. View along courtyard towards the lake. Movable wood frame, with sun shading on hotel facade
141. Hotel La Angostura. View from the lake towards the hotel
142. Hotel La Angostura. Bar/reception/lounge at entry area

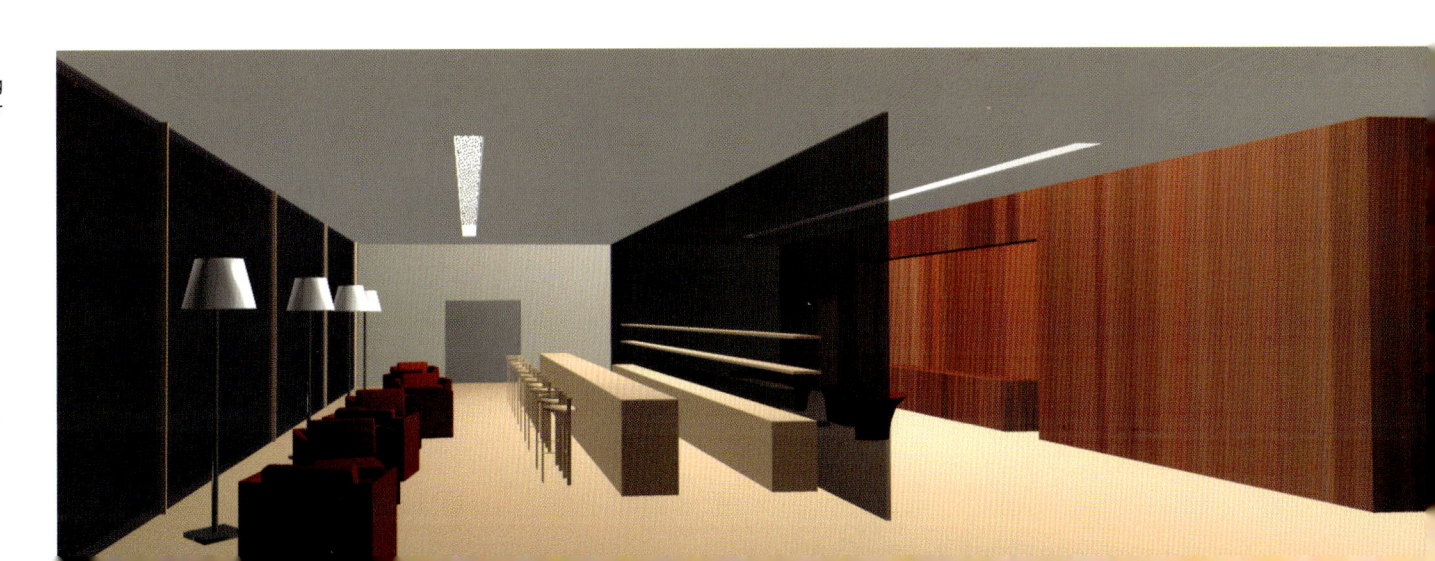

143. Hotel La Angostura. Interior of hotel's observation room loking towards opening to the outdoor viewing deck
144. Hotel La Angostura. Interior of observation room looking towards entry
145. Hotel La Angostura. View from the lake towards the main building on the left and bungalows on the right, with viewing deck at from of main building, in wood and concrete
146. Hotel La Angostura. Bar/reception/lounge at entry area

Stephen Alton Architect, P.C.: Firm Profile

RETAIL

Donna Karan Beauty
Prototype Design, Fixture Design,
Store Planning and Design
Macy's Herald Square, NYC, NY
Bloomingdale's, NYC, NY
Macy's, Fox Hills Mall, Culver City, CA
Macy's Union Square, San Francisco, CA
Liberty House, Ala Moana, HI
Harvey Nichols, London, England

DK Home
Prototype Design and Fixture Design

Donna Karan Menswear / DKNY / Donna Karan Collection
Store Design and Fixture Design
Al Amoudi, Jeddah, Saudi Arabia

Donna Karan Intimates
Prototype Design, Fixture Design,
Store Planning and Design
Macy's Herald Square, NYC, NY
Macy's, Beverly Center, Los Angeles, CA
Bloomingdale's, NYC, NY

Chaps Ralph Lauren
Prototype Design, Fixture Design, and Store Planning
Macy's Herald Square, NYC, NY

Genesco / Journeys Shoes
Prototype Design, Fixture Design,
Signage and Packaging Design

Royale Cards and Gifts
Store Design and Fixture Design
177 West 4th Street, NYC, NY

Danone International Brands
Temporary Exhibition Design for Food Products
(Danone Yogurt, Evian Water, Volvic Water, Lu Cookies, Lea & Perrins)
Marriott Copley Square, Boston, MA

Sacco Shoes
Prototype Design, Fixture Design, and Store Planning
94 Seventh Avenue, NYC, NY
45 East 17th Street, NYC, NY
324 Columbus Avenue, NYC, NY
2355 Broadway, NYC, NY

Nancy Geist Shoes
Store design, exterior work, and Landmarks approvals for the oldest building in Soho
107 Spring Street, NYC, NY

Ligne Roset Furniture Store
Store design and selection of furniture for sales floor
Westport, CT

Mare Shoes
Store design and Landmarks approvals
100 Fifth Avenue, NYC, NY

OFFICES

Violy, Byorum and Partners Offices
6,500 SF Corporate Office of Investment Counseling Organization
712 Fifth Avenue, NYC, NY

John Weiser MD
Doctors' Offices
NYC, NY

Soho Pediatrics
Doctors' Offices
NYC, NY

Dr. Brian Meehan
Doctors' Offices
NYC, NY

MULTI-UNIT RESIDENTIAL

Nicole
A Gotham Construction Development. Residential Lobby and Public Areas, Exterior Building Development Consultation, Interior Design (lobby, health club/gymnasium, lounge, public corridors, mail room, elevators). 400 West 55th St, NYC

Atlas New York
A Gotham Construction Development. Residential Lobby and Public Areas, Business Lobby, Exterior Building Development Consultation, Interior Design (lobby, health club/gymnasium, lounge, public corridors, mail room, elevators). 47-Floor 375-Unit Apartment Building. 66 W. 38th Str, NYC

New Gotham
A Gotham Construction Development. Lobby and Public Area Design, Exterior Building Development Consultation, Entry Canopy Design, Interior Design (lobby, basketball gymnasium, health club, lounges, public corridors, elevators), Model apartment interior design and furnishings for 34-Floor 375-Unit Apartment Building. 520 West 43rd Street, NYC

Hudson Place
Model Apartments, NYC

Hudson Tea Building
A Donaldson, Lufkin, & Jenrette Development Hudson Tea Building. Model Apartments, Rental Offices, Lobbies and Public Areas. Hoboken, NJ

Tribeca Bridge Tower
Model Apartments and Rental Offices Battery Park City Residential Complex

New Hudson Waterfront Building
A Joint Venture between Hudson Waterfront Associates, L.P., and the Trump Organization.
Model Apartments

Hudson Tea Building "A"
Planning, Base Building Architecture, Interior Design. Hoboken, N.J.

The Marais
The Hudson Companies Inc. Model Apartments, NYC

River Place ILLC
A Silverstein Properties Development. Model Apartments for 33-Floor Apartment Building 42nd Street and Twelfth Avenue, NYC

146-148 West 22nd Street
Interior Design, Lobby and 12 condominium units. Alchemy Properties, NYC

Avalon Bay Communities
Residential Lobby and Public Areas, Unit interiors materials selection, Gym, lounge, mailroom, concierge, public corridors, elevators. A 200 unit Apartment building. Houston Street, NYC

Cambridge Companies
Facade design, Residential Lobby and Public Areas, Gym, lounge, swimming area, mail room, concierge, public corridors, elevators. A 200-unit Condominium building. 59th and West End Avenue, NYC

RESTAURANTS AND HOSPITALITY

Excelsior Restaurant
Architecture and Interior Design for 6,500 SF Restaurant and Gourmet Take-Out in New Construction
Hackensack, NJ

Hotel Adagio
Representation for Owner (CSFB)
SAA was team leader in the development of Architectural and Interior design direction for a 370 room hotel that included restaurant and complete hotel renovation
Geary Street, San Francisco, CA

Hudson Hotel
Ian Schrager Hotels Inc.
Redesign of floor configurations, suite development, and enlargement of typical single and double rooms. Model room design and development and construction drawings for renovation.
NYC, NY

Hotel Wales
Lobby and executive suite renovation
Madison Avenue, NYC, NY

Ritz-Carlton San Juan Puerto
Restaurant Design (two), public lobby and lounge bar, architectural addition to veranda bar areas
San Juan, Puerto Rico

PRIVATE RESIDENCES

Seidmon Residence
NYC, NY

Young-Mallin Residence
NYC, NY

Carlson Residence
East Village, NYC, NY

Carlson Residence
West Village, NYC, NY

Moses Residence
NYC, NY

Carlson Residence
Miami, Florida

Krug-Haubrich Residence
East Hampton, NY

Dlutowski-Occolowitz Residence
NYC, NY

Luke Residence
NYC, NY

Stephen Alton Architect, P.C., www.stephenalton.com
Firm Profile

AWARDS / TELEVISION / PUBLICATIONS / ACADEMICS

Television Feature
　Terrance Conran's on Design, April 1996
ID Awards
　Honorable mention for Royale Cards, July-August 1996
Parsons School of Design
　Visiting Faculty, Fall 1996
Metropolitan Home
　Seidmon Residence, November 1996
House and Garden
　Mallen Residence, January 1997
Home Office Book
　Mallen Residence Office, March 1997
NY City Life
　Seidmon Residence, Fall 1997
Interior Design
　Sacco Shoes, April 1998
New York Sunday Times
　Tribeca Bridge Towers, November 1999
Flatiron Magazine
　Feature on SAA, April 1999
Interior Design
　New Gotham, October 1999
Interior Design
　Ligne Roset, May 2000
House Beautiful
　Ligne Roset, June 2000
Elle
　Nancy Geist, September 2000
Real Estate News
　New Gotham, September 2000
Lighting Design Awards
　Lumen Award for New Gotham, Year 2000
Woman's Wear Daily
　Atlas, June 2002
New York Sunday Times
　Atlas, July 2002
Fox 5 News
　Atlas, September 2002
Stone World
　Atlas, March 2003
Architectural Record
　Atlas, May 2003
Hamptons Cottages and Gardens
　Krug Haubrich Residence, August 2003
Arhitext Design
　Livio Dimitriu feature on SAA: Bodies of Space and Tattooed Skins, September/October 2003
Arhitext Design
　Dlutowski & Occolowitz, November 2003
Arhitext Design
　Feature of SAA Interior Design, December 2003
Arhitext Design
　Atlas, cover and article, January 2004
Arhitext Design
　The Hudson Tea Building "A," June 2004

STEPHEN ALTON / ARCHITECTURE: BODIES OF SPACE

Stephen Alton Architect, P.C., www.stephenalton.com
Firm Profile

CREDITS

Atlas New York
Project Leader: Michael McNeil. Project Interior Designer: Masako Fukuoka. Lighting Consultant: Focus Lighting. Light wall by: Amanda Weill. Cabinetry in lounge: Steve Iino

New Gotham
Project Leader: Kenneth Abrams. Lighting Designer: Gary Gordon

Hudson Hotel
Project Leader: Masako Fukuoka. Team Members: Richard Stucki, Ade Herkarisma

Mare Shoes
Project Leader: Michael McNeil. Woodwork: Steve Lino. Lighting Consultant: Focus Lighting

Donna Karan
Project Leader: Jason Kreuzer. Lighting Consultant: Johnson and Schwinghammer

Royale Cards and Gifts
None

Sacco Shoes
Kenneth Abrams

Ligne Roset
Michael McNeil

Apt. 22
Michael McNeil

Apt. 11
Kenneth Abrams, colorist Eve Ashcroft. Bathroom and kitchen finishes: Art In Construction

Dual Space: Seidmon Residence
Kenneth Abrams

House Addition: Art Port / Krug and
Project Leader: Michael McNeil. Project Interior Designer: Masako Fukuoka

Haubrich
Michael McNeil

Concept Restaurant
Michael McNeil

Astor
Project Leader: Michael McNeil, with Ron Mack Ade Herkarisma

Hotel Villa La Angostura
Michael McNeil, Richard Stucki

Hoboken Building "A"
Ade Herkarisma

Soho Med
Michael McNiel, Richard Stucki

USA BOOKS | UNIVERSALIA PUBLISHERS
New York / Verona / Bucharest